Game Warden Gone Rogue

How the Washington Dept. of Fish and Wildlife Compel Outdoor Enthusiasts to CHEAT

Shame on the progressive minded politicians who flood the world with new laws and at the same time destroy our abilities to enforce them. Ignominy is due those that emphasize the "best available science," then twist bad science to suit them, and use it for their monetary, political or personal interests. Disgraceful are those WDFW commissioners and managers who place the outdoor enthusiast at risk of criminal or civil prosecution due to their own indifference.

Gregory F. Haw

Washington Fish and Wildlife Officer (Retired)

ISBN: 9798360016694

Old friends doing something that is very unlawful now.

Dear Fish and Wildlife Officers who may read this book:

I write this with a great deal of trepidation. The F&W regulations have been messed up for many years. The real victims are you, and the hunters and fishers of the great state of Washington. Some of you may take offense to what I say here.

Understandably so. However my intent is not to diminish your contribution to the natural world, but to improve upon it. This goal can be sooner reached if fishing and hunting regulations made sense. Currently they do not. I have been highly compelled to write about your plight. I have waited three years since retirement to do so. I can wait no longer

If what I write causes you grief, I am sorry. My intent is to protect you. You have already paid enough with the risks and abuses that you take, as well as with unreasonable police reform laws. What I say here may seem like an addition to your burden.

I am certain you can handle it. I ask only that each and every one of you seek out ways to improve upon, and to simplify, hunting and fishing regulations. You are the only ones who know all of the issues, until now.

Game Warden / Fish Cop forever, and with much love.

Your old pal Greg

CONTENTS

Disclaimer

The author is not an attorney. Thoughts expressed within this document are the beliefs of a lay person with no expertise in law. They are opinions, beliefs, and yes, a few guesses only. These thoughts are based on the author's experience, mostly at the district court level. Do not consider this document legal advice. Some of the anecdotal descriptions are partially fictitious, and used to make a point, however all are plausible and reflect the opinion and memory of the author. Some names have been changed, although they may represent real people.

Gregory F. Haw

A FOREWORD BY THE HONORABLE

GARY W. VELIE

Clallam County Superior Court Judge. Former Deputy, Fish and Wildlife Officer (Retired) and salmon fisherman.

I was appointed to the bench as a Superior Court Judge in 1983 by Governor John Spellman. I lost a bid for re-election in 1992 and started my Law Enforcement career. I finished the Reserve Academy and volunteered with the Clallam County Sheriff Office as a Reserve Deputy and eventually applied for a vacancy, was accepted and attended the Criminal Justice Training Center Basic Law Enforcement Academy. I worked as a Patrol Deputy in Clallam County and as a Marine Law Enforcement officer each summer. I was eventually assigned as a Recreational Deputy and worked half of my time with a WDFW Officer doing Enforcement work and Greg worked with me doing Marine and Recreational Patrol duties. I retired in 2005 and was offered a job with WDFW as an Enforcement Officer. I worked full time July through November and then parked the truck and did not start until the July of the following year. I finally retired for real 2009. The WDFW is the epitome of an agency that tries, in theory, to actually preserve habitat, wildlife and the fisheries for the benefit of Washington's citizens. The pamphlet (actually an entire book) that seeks to lay out the rules and regulations for the recreational fisherman is a travesty! When I was stationed in Florida, I observed that the state has a tremendous fishery and their rules pamphlet is extremely thin and easily read and understood. The same cannot be said for Washington. Ours is a monstrosity that tries and fails

miserably to lay out the regulations and rules in any way that can be read and understood by the average person.

Greg has gone to great lengths to explain the continuous contradictions and outright errors that are never corrected in subsequent editions even after they have been brought to the attention of the people responsible for the content of this publication. These pamphlets contain the "laws and rules" that the Enforcement Officers (now Police) are required to enforce. This book points out why Greg has "gone rogue" and shows it for the totally ridiculous tool that it is. Anyone new to the state or a visiting vacationer would absolutely not be able to use this pamphlet to understand the requirements and comply well enough to avoid a citation if stopped and inspected.

Any trial of a Criminal charge would be almost impossible to be ethically conducted given the requirement of proof beyond a reasonable doubt. In spite of these flaws, I remain an angler as I have been a Washington resident for 80 years, except for the several years of active military service.

Gary W. Velie

(1)

PREFACE

Game Warden Gone Rogue

How the Washington Department of Fish and Wildlife compel outdoor enthusiasts to cheat

BY Greg Haw F&W Officer Retired

Motivated entirely by impossible to follow, let alone understand, recreational fishing and hunting regulations in the great state of Washington, I sit down to make a few points. In two prior books, I have attempted to express the ludicrous way in which the state of Washington controls the take of their precious natural resources. It was my intent to point this out to the powers that be. All efforts fell upon deaf ears. It is with an act of desperation, and not without a great deal of trepidation, that I begin once again.

My sole purpose is to educate the so called "experts," regarding real world problems with the associated regulations that need to be fixed. I will be doing so with some hypotheticals. Although many enclosed examples happened on my watch, I assure you, all scenarios are very plausible and could easily happen. (Many are happening as we read.)

I give to the reader my experiences and opinions compiled during a lifetime of hunting and fishing. I include experience based upon thirty nine years with the state of Washington Department of Fish and Wildlife, including thirty four years as a wildlife enforcement officer.

To many recreational hunters and fishers, both living and visiting Washington State, I humbly apologize for my failure to improve recreational hunting and fishing laws on my tour of duty.

I will be focusing of the Revised Code of Washington (RCW). The Washington Administrative Code (WAC), and particularly on the Washington Department of Fish and Wildlife, Sport Fishing Rules pamphlet, 2021-22.

Do I suffer from misplaced catholic guilt? Perhaps, or do I seek amends, atonement, forgiveness, or absolution? I don't know, but I have to get some things off my chest!

There are many victims of "bad regulations," not the least of which are the natural resources that they are designed to protect and the law enforcement professionals that enforce them. The recreational angler/hunter, thousands of whom are afraid to pursue their passion for fear of unknowingly committing a violation are victimized. The overall quality of an outdoor pursuit, something that attracts many to the Pacific Northwest, is obviously affected. Close to my heart, is the effect it has on the men and women of the wildlife enforcement program, all of whom care deeply for the natural world. Bad fish and wildlife regulations, which are not their fault, place them in harm's way. They already have plenty of other things to worry about due to recent police reform laws.

It is inevitable for them, that at some point in their career, they will have to use force while enforcing laws that are ambiguous and that their superiors clearly don't care about. They have my prayers.

Hunter / angler for life...Gregory F. Haw

(2)

Good idea but poorly thought out

Once upon a time a **WDFW** ground fish biologist became interested in shore bound rockfish and lingcod fishing occurring on several jetties on the Washington coast. He was no doubt so interested that he tried it himself. After a great day of catching numerous black rockfish and a large lingcod he started his hazardous hike back the way he came. The only possible route was over huge and very inconveniently placed rip rap boulders stretching for over half a mile. Nearly breaking a leg numerous times, he and his 50 pound catch of whole fish, finally made it back to the truck. He did not fillet out his catch out on the jetty, something that would have made his trek far more pleasant, not to mention safer. The fishing regulations prohibited it! There are bag and size limits with many different species involved. Filleting fish in the field makes it more difficult for enforcement officers to enforce these rules. At the time, an angler could be cited for mutilating his catch in the field because it made identification, counting and measuring difficult.

"I need to do something before an angler gets hurt or dies trying to fish here," the well-meaning biologist said to himself. *"Somethings got to be done."*

Sure enough, this guy was in a position to change what appeared to him to be a silly law. He played a few word games with the regulations and the next year things changed. The new law, that remains in effect today says, *"Once a shore bound angler is done fishing for the day, he may process his catch in the field."* Less burdened by the bulk of his catch, the jetty angler arrived home safely. The result being, a fairly unpopular fishery became more popular and far safer. Great job! Or was it?

Right about the same time, wild steelhead and salmon populations went into a tailspin. Wild fish release became the norm. Does this law intended for shore bound ground fish anglers apply to the walk in steelhead angler on the upper Hoh River or any other place where wild fish need protection? Yes it does! Wild steelhead are distinguished by an intact adipose fin. This fin almost always disappears during the act of filleting and is discarded in the process. Can an enforcement officer distinguish an unlawful wild fish from a lawful hatchery fish if cut into steaks and inside a backpack? Of course not!

Even though it is imperative that wild fish are protected, it is now perfectly lawful for a steelhead angler to do this, as long as he or she is, *"shore bound and done fishing for the day."* (This does not apply to boat anglers, where lawful fish must be retained whole.)

Clearly the regulation allowing the field processing of fish on the jetty, should not apply where wild salmon steelhead protection measures are in place. But it does!

What applies to the shore bound lingcod angler and the steelhead angler should be the same...or at least clarified. Management is fully aware of this legal contradiction. I know because I told them. I'll bet that the current Wildlife Commission remains totally in the dark on the matter.

Unlawful wild fish, disguised to look like lawful hatchery fish.

(3)

When is a fishing license required?

While training new officers, I was constantly asking hypothetical questions. Not to humiliate the student, as some believed, but in an attempt to determine where training should be concentrated. The regulation pamphlet, with all its constant changes, errors and nonsensical language, was a huge burden to this process. One question told me a lot about where a new officer was in his training. The question was:

"In what situations does an angler in Washington State need not present a fishing license?"

It's not a straight forward question. Few student officers correctly answered it. *The answers are:*

1) No license required on free fishing weekend. (But one still needs a catch record card when fishing crab, sturgeon, salmon, steelhead, halibut, and a license is required to have one of those!)
2) No license required for juveniles, but catch record cards are required.
3) No license is required in National Parks…but catch record cards are and a license is still required on park beaches. (Go figure)
4) No license required for freshwater smelt fishing. (Few alive remember why.)
5) No license required to fish for carp. (Although a documented food fish in Washington, no one, including me, knows why!)

6) A treaty tribal member, while executing his or her treaty fishing rights, within his or her ceded area, does not need any sort of state license or catch record card.
7) Recreational license required, only when fishing for personal use.

Let's take a look at answer number five. Within in it exists a loophole, effecting a license requirement for many freshwater bodies of water in Washington.

Common carp were introduced into North America throughout the 1860s. They became established in the lower Columbia River by about 1880. A small but viable commercial fishery for them was established. They have since expanded throughout the state of Washington, particularly in the vast Columbia River basin, to now include virtually every lowland body of water in eastern Washington. In 1967, 1.2 million pounds of carp were taken from Banks Lake alone. Western Washington is now home for them too, and carp inhabit many bodies of water including much of the Chehalis River basin.

Carp are considered a great eating, hard fighting sport fish in large parts of the world. Only in America is the term *"trash fish"* applied to them. Any true fly fisherman knows that a carp will bite nearly any fly in his massive assortment of flies, if presented with skill and great patience. Many a small boy, like me for example, were thrilled when a large carp decided to swallow a grasshopper intended for a trout. A 15 pound carp, or an 8 inch rainbow trout? The choice for me was obvious and remains so.

Experience has taught me that carp will take nearly any small organic material as food, including angle worms, periwinkles, snails, any nymph like fly, or even soft plastic *"artificial"* baits designed for bass, crappie, sunfish and perch. My point being, if an enforcement officer sees one fishing in this manner, does the angler need a fishing license if fishing in a body of water where carp occur? Well, the answer is that the burden of proof as to what the angler is fishing for is carried by the enforcing officer. He or she must prove beyond a reasonable doubt what species the angler was seeking at the moment observed. The angler does not have to prove anything. In other words, the officer must know what the angler was thinking. In my opinion, because clearly a license is not required to fish for carp, the officer must assume that the angler is fishing for carp, unless the angler says otherwise, or is in possession of other fish species.

Many fresh water *"fishing without a license"* citations could be negated because of the carp fishing loophole.

How about a law that reads: *"Any overt attempt to capture a fish in state waters, regardless of method used, or fish species sought, requires a license, with the exception of juveniles, treaty fishers lawfully applying treaty fishing rights, or fishing on free fishing weekend."*

Similarly, a recreational license is not required to fish for smelt in fresh water. Most people know smelt by the Columbia River version that swim up the Cowlitz River in February each year. They are recreationally and commercially *"dipped"* with hand held nets when abundance justifies an open fishery. They certainly could be caught on hook and line if an angler used small baits or artificial lures. Jigging, effectively snagging them, would also work. That method is widely used in Puget Sound in order to harvest their saltwater cousins. *(Surf smelt.)*

Back in about 1985, the Washington Department of Fisheries and the Washington legislature imposed a *"Personal Use Fishing License."* It made a great deal of sense, because prior to this law, no license of any kind was required for *"food fish"* except a catch record card was required for salmon. This proposed law was opposed by an elected official in southwest Washington, who argued that his constituents should not need a license to dip smelt. In an effort to get the new law passed, the license for smelt requirement was dropped. However, a much needed $3 personal use license was adopted for all other species of food fish, except carp. Even though Columbia River Smelt are now listed as *"threatened"* under the Endangered Species Act, and demand a great deal of attention, public funds, enforcement attention, and management efforts, there now remains this law. Why surf smelt fishers are exempted from a license requirement is anyone's guess.

As if the regulations could not get any worse, I discovered another interesting fishing licensing loophole. A license is only required if one is fishing for *"personal use."*

"Angling" is defined on page 18 of the current recreational sport fishing rules pamphlet as: *Fishing for personal use, not for trade, barter or sale, with a line attached to a pole capable of being held in hand while landing fish, or a hand-operated line without a rod or reel. (Inexplicably, this same definition of angling gear would apply to a conventional gaff hook and its use.)*

That means to me, and probably to any District Court in Washington, that if a person is fishing for someone else, donations to a food bank, or for trade, barter or sale, an angler need not have a recreational fishing license. The catch would be that he would need a commercial fishing license if planning to sell food fish. What a fool the fish cop would be to charge the rod and reel angler with a Class C felony! (Unbelievably, that was the advice I once received from a supervisor when discussing this scenario.)

A much smaller point is that the term *"pole"* and *"rod"* are both used in the same sentence, suggesting that they are different things.

Even the simplest of fishing violations is thus rendered highly questionable by regulation language that is totally ambiguous and unnecessary.

The WDFW is largely dependent upon license sales for operating revenue. I can't tell you how many times managers have announced proposed license fee increases by exclaiming *"We haven't had a license fee increase in X number of years."* They conveniently forget other imposed costs that appear in the form of special endorsements, Columbia River salmon, Puget Sound crab endorsement (winter/summer,) seaweed, two pole endorsements, and the like. (They truly think that we are not on to them.)

These same folks are totally ignorant of the fact that enforcing any fishing license mandate becomes problematic due to their sloppy approach to license requirements in the first place. The enforcement officer must be able to sort through this and many other apparent ambiguities, they should not have to do so.

"A state is better governed which has few laws, and those laws strictly observed." (Rene Descartes)

Happy carp anglers. No license required!

(4)

Possession of live wildlife (angle worms)

If one were to closely examine fishing regulations in Washington State, he or she is in for many surprises. According to the Revised Code of Washington (RCW) and the Washington Administrative Code (WAC), it is unlawful to possess, *"live"* wildlife without a permit from the director. Defined in RCW 77.08.010 (72) and detailed in WAC 220-450-030, this includes *"all animal species that occur in Washington in a wild state."* Even non-native, exotic and often *"invasive"* species live in a *"wild state"* in Washington. (Interestingly, RCW 16 defines wildlife differently.)

There are many examples of well-established exotic species: Green crab, Pacific oysters, Manilla clams, Varnish clams, Eurasian collard doves, European starlings, English house sparrow, feral cats, rats, opossums, virtually all warm water gamefish, bullfrogs, and many species of game birds. The list goes on and on. Oh yes, this list includes the common angle worm.

The common angle worm was introduced into North America by, you guessed it, immigrant gardeners. Enriching the soil in a largely agrarian culture was important, and highly beneficial. Negative impacts include a change in soil chemistry that has been proven to negatively affect some native forests however, but most results were positive. One, especially important to me is, as their common name implies, they make great fishing bait! And yes, they *"live in a wild state!"*

The term *"drowning a worm"* means *"A slow fishing day."* To any angler, the term, *"hand me another worm,"* means *"hand me another bait."* Angle worms are so closely associated with recreational fishing that nearly any bait or lure is referred to by anglers as a worm!

Preparation is required for even the most simple of fishing trips. Almost all new anglers learned quickly how to dig in the soil or to hunt night crawlers with a flashlight. Most budding anglers know that especially fat angle worms are conveniently found under a properly aged cow pie. Catching bait is a large part of the fun for a novice, typically a young angler. We are all technically criminal's! WDFW regulations appear to outlaw the possession of angle worms! Trafficking Live Wildlife, that means selling night crawlers, by extension, could be interpreted as a potentially felony level crime!

Forget about using grasshoppers, crickets, maggots, and periwinkles, even highly destructive crane fly larva, for bait too!

Furthermore, many rural kids as well as grade school students in urban areas, learn about the facts of life by watching tadpoles develop from egg to frog. For me, that *"pickle jar"* science experiment was earth moving. It started my unending interest in natural processes and laid down the foundation for a career in fish and wildlife protection. I'm sure that many scientists were similarly inspired. Are we all criminals too?

In my opinion few higher ups in the WDFW are aware of these things, but, they are not shy about saying, *"We must work with the best available science."* This begs the question: *"What does their worst available science look like?"*

It is not a stretch of current law to interpret that such prohibitions exist in an enforceable form, and could be abused by anti-hunting and anti-fishing political groups. Especially those trying to limit our outdoor opportunities. Perhaps, even by the WDFW commission and those anti-hunting and fishing advocates that advise them.

"It is impossible to tell where the law stops and justice begins." *(Earl Warren)*

Trust me kids. They **WILL** turn into frogs! Sorry, it's a crime to show you.

Good Data vs. Bad Data

Early in my career I collected salmon and ground fish catch data at numerous sea ports. Anglers were interviewed, marked fish were meticulously measured, and the data was used to measure take, the lack thereof, and / or overall participation in the fishery. I was taught from an early point: *"There are only two kinds of data, good and bad. Bad data destroys the value of good data therefore it makes all data worthless."*

Nowadays, **WDFW** port samplers also collect data regarding a myriad of other things, including the time anglers started, finished, what species were encountered, and more. One thing that they seem particularly interested in is the number of *"wild fish released." (Known as encounters.)*

This is a good question because a mortality factor is applied to wild fish encountered by anglers. If hooked and released a percentage die and are added to the number of fish taken. Even if a fish is hooked momentarily, and comes off, another mortality factor is imposed called *"drop off."* This information is intended for one purpose: Fish released, and those that *"drop off,"* represent a percentage of dead wild fish. When this anticipated number is reached the season is closed via an emergency order. Almost all anglers know this! Furthermore, the anglers' distrust of **WDFW** management is so widespread, they rightfully believe that a truthful answer to these questions cuts their season short!

When I was checked at the Port Angeles boat ramp in July of 2021 my partners and I came in with a limit of six chinook. It was a great day! Of course we released a number of nice un-marked fish too. When I truthfully answered the fish sampler's question, one could have heard a pin drop. I got the *"hairy eyeball"* from everyone within ear shot. I heard a guy mutter, loud enough for all to hear say, *"That guy is an idiot, he must be from out of town. Doesn't he know that they're just going to shut the season down sooner?"*

If WDFW thinks that they are getting usable data at popular sea ports by asking that question, their office must be on Mars!

WDFW also applies a mortality factor to released *"wild steelhead."* Similarly, releasing any fish involves a percentage of loss called *"hooking mortality."* To my knowledge the mortality factor used is completely arbitrary and has not been sufficiently studied. What I find strange, and difficult to understand, is that there is a known mortality rate on hook and line caught wild steelhead from brood stock hook-and-line collection projects. When WDFW targets wild steelhead with rod and reel, for brood stock, the mortality rate *"magically"* falls well below levels associated with recreational fishing. (These losses are deemed acceptable, according to them, in spite of the fact that steelhead so collected are handled far more extensively than those released in a sport fishery)

I once confronted a WDFW regional manager regarding this clear contradiction. He was one of the employees that enthusiastically, and recreationally, participated in this hook-and-line project. He told me, *"The brood stock fish are all killed for spawning, therefore the mortality rate is 100 percent. Now get out of my office."* That my friends, represents how much fish managers respect the input of dumb fish cops.

Always remember that the dumb fish cop is on your side, despite what you see with your own eyes.

In this day and age, bad data is primarily used to make a talking point, to deflect argument and more often it seems, in an attempt to outright deceive. We are bombarded by it! Data is collected, distorted and manipulated by all sides of present day hot button issues, especially fisheries management. This trend is rampant when discussing pandemics, race relations in America, climate change and even employment numbers. Yet this (fake news) concept is conspicuously ignored by today's media.

Fisheries science is largely number crunching and identifying trends. Politicalized fish management is all about manipulating numbers and manufacturing trends, sometimes for hidden reasons.

Remember, even a baseball player who hits 300 against righties, oftentimes can't hit a southpaw! One talent scout can argue that he is a poor hitter, another that he is great! The fact is, the hitter must be wisely used, depending upon who is pitching. Statistics can be twisted any way one wishes.

"Lies, damned lies and statistics." Is a phrase describing the pervasive power of statistics to bolster weak arguments. It is also sometimes colloquially used to doubt statistics used to prove an opponent's point. (Cornelius Jabez Hughes)

(6)

Largemouth and Smallmouth bass regulations

These two species are the most sought-after game fish in North America. Although not native to the Pacific Northwest, their populations have exploded, particularly that of smallmouth. Huge populations have established throughout the state, much to the deterrent of native salmon populations. Despite this well-known negative impact, bass have been protected for years by bag and slot limits. (Slot limits are retention size restrictions with both a minimum and maximum consideration.)

A well know example involves sturgeon with a 43 inch minimum size and a 52 inch maximum. An angler must hit the slot, in order to retain the fish. Another example involves bass. The limit may be five fish with only one to be retained over 14 inches in length. This does not matter to the bass anglers because they tend to be great advocates of catch and release, an enviable ethic also practiced by most fly fishermen.

Unfortunately for salmon, bass tend to thrive in areas where juvenile salmon rear. Bass voraciously feed upon juvenile salmon, particularly *"wild chinook."* Their impact upon salmon stocks has finally been recognized by WDFW and bass retention laws have been somewhat liberalized recently.

When this issue was coming to a head I had a friendly conversation with a regional fish manager, I'll call him Jerry. In a prior position with WDFW he was a warm water fish specialist working with bass, crappie and such. I argued that bass limits needed to be liberalized to reduce impacts on salmon, particularly in the nearby Chehalis River basin. I advised him that Smallmouth bass were taking over. He reminded me of his expertise with bass, and had published papers regarding other warm water species. What he said to me left me speechless! He said that the only predator on small bass was that of large bass, therefore, we need to protect the large bass to keep the small ones in check. I mumbled something like, *"What about the wild fish that sportsmen have to release, bass eat those too!"* Jerry's statement, if presented to a group of bass anglers would have been met with a standing ovation! Salmon anglers would have booed him out of the ballpark. Anyhow, he left me feeling totally out of touch. I was so shocked about what he said, I recorded it in my daily log book.

Fast forward two years, bass predation on salmon became a major issue. Retention limits on bass were liberalized, much to the chagrin of bass anglers, but to the applause of salmon anglers. It was a good decision, but not nearly aggressive enough. Bass fishing is as good as ever.

After retirement I was having a friendly Facebook conversation with Jerry. This same subject came up. Without thinking I reminded him of the position he took several years prior. He got angry. He said he had never uttered something so absurd and that wild salmon were a far higher priority. *"I never said such a thing!"* Taken aback, shocked if you will, I told him that there were witnesses to this conversation and that I had recorded it in my officer's log. I don't recall his exact words but he essentially called me a liar and abruptly terminated the conversation.

Now I was angry! Facebook is no way to communicate but my integrity had been challenged. I was new to Facebook so I asked my wife how to *"unfriend"* someone. *"No problem. Give me your phone."* Try as she may, she could not figure out how. It turned out that Jerry had already unfriended me!

Is regulatory input accepted by the *"boots on the ground"* enforcement officer with thirty nine years of service? No! Is management open to any form of constructive criticism? Never!

"It is certain, in any case, that ignorance allied with power is the most ferocious enemy justice can have." (James Baldwin)

7

Wild fish paradox and "reasonable doubt"

For many years the highlight of my summer was patrolling the Skokomish River in Mason County Washington. Supplied by a highly productive WDFW Salmon Hatchery, thousands of beautiful fall chinook returned each year, often as early as the 4th of July. A hugely popular fishery developed.

To intentionally snag a salmon is a crime. It is defined by any attempt to impale a fish on a hook without the fish biting the bait or lure. This violation was easy to enforce until some well-meaning, but very detached biologist, came into the picture and created the *"anti-snagging rules."* These new regulations only served to muddy the waters and make the enforcement officer's job far more difficult.

 Ironically, due directly to *"anti-snagging rules,"* it is lawful to snag a fish in fresh water if the fish is hooked on or near the head. The act of *"flossing"* was born, much to the chagrin of the conscientious angler. This technically unlawful act was made simple by the crystal clear, and very low waters, of the Skokomish River, which is typical of summer flows in most salmon streams.

We officers worked the hell out of it. We often had plain clothed officers fishing at strategic locations calling out violations as they saw them. Stone faced fish cops, myself included, would often appear out of concealment and make very righteous pinches. That got old after a while so we often focused on *"wild fish"* retention, which was, and remains, unlawful in most areas.

As most anglers know, a wild fish is defined, for regulatory purposes, by one that has an intact adipose fin. Those with a clipped or missing fin are lawful to retain. In addition, one must also be aware that a *"wild fish"* case is far more important than that of simple snagging.

I must also point out that the court may impose upon the violator, jail of up to one year, a $5,000 fine, forfeiture of equipment used, a strike against their fishing license privileges, and a criminal record! In addition the court of jurisdiction <u>must</u> impose a $500 *"criminal assessment penalty"* for the loss of each fish.

Now consider this. Little known to the angling public, as many as ten percent of hatchery fish produced and released are intentionally not fin clipped. Many of these are in fact fitted with a coded wire tag, injected into the snout. Easily proven to be of hatchery origin, they remain defined as *"wild"* because they have an intact adipose fin and are protected as such.

Now consider this: **RCW 77.15.370**

Unlawful recreational fishing in the first degree—Penalty—Criminal wildlife penalty assessment.

(1) A person is guilty of unlawful recreational fishing in the first degree if:

(g)(i) The person possesses a wild salmon or wild steelhead during a season closed for wild salmon or wild steelhead.

(ii) For the purposes of this subsection:

(A) "Wild salmon" means a salmon with an unclipped adipose fin, regardless of whether the salmon's ventral fin is clipped. A salmon is considered to have an unclipped adipose fin if it

does not have a healed scar at the location of the clipped adipose fin.

    (c) Wild salmon or wild steelhead, five hundred dollars.

    (4) If two or more persons are convicted under subsection (1) of this section, and subsection (3) of this section is applicable, the criminal wildlife penalty assessment must be imposed against the persons jointly and severally.

    (5)(a) The criminal wildlife penalty assessment under subsection (3) of this **section must be imposed regardless of and in addition to any sentence, fines, or costs otherwise provided for violating any provision of this section**. The criminal wildlife penalty assessment must be included by the court in any pronouncement of sentence and may not be suspended, waived, modified, or deferred in any respect.

The Department of Fish and Wildlife, admits that many hatchery produced fish are not marked, then in the next breath defines millions of what they know to be hatchery fish as *"wild."* Ask yourself, how can the state impose penalties this severe, if they are fully aware of, and intentionally see to it, that at least ten percent of the so called *"wild fish"* are in fact of hatchery origin? My god, who do they think they are?

What would the salmon angler think if he was aware that 10 percent (at least) of the hatchery fish that he paid to produce were off limits to him? He may want his license money back! It is no wonder that there are so many conspiracy theorists out there!

One day, on the Skokomish River, while suffering a case of writer's cramp and training a new officer, I decided to visit my old colleagues at the George Adams Salmon Hatchery. The crew was working hard, sorting fish and loading them up on a truck. They explained to me that the hatchery had gotten far more fish than needed and that the agency was selling **our** surplus chinook to a buyer.

Now, for the moment, forget the obvious, that many anglers would have loved to have caught these fish. What I saw was unbelievable! Unclipped, and what the state had defined as protected wild fish, unlawful to possess by anglers, were getting loaded up onto a surplus truck! Yes, the very same fish, that I had been taking significant risk protecting not 30 minutes prior!

Quite frankly, I could not in any way justify what appeared to be an obvious conflict of interest to my impressionable student officer. I was personally, deeply embarrassed. Once again, everything that I was trying to teach, namely, enforcement and biological priorities, were rendered null and void by some cubical bound salmon manager completely unconcerned with integrity, credibility or common sense.

Often anglers are required to release fish that are, in fact, of hatchery origin. Partial clips, deformed fins, missed clips and even regenerated adipose fins, (commonly encountered), all serve to confuse anglers and fish cops alike. While training new officers I always had them serve time in the *"clipping trailer"* in order to make this point. The student officer's work was evaluated and their failure rate was documented.

This attempt to provide perspective often did not work. Later, when assigned a different training officer, students would cite anglers for possessing unclipped fish when in fact the fish were *"partially"* clipped. Student officers that had an angling background performed far better.

Even some naturally reproducing stocks of hatchery fish do very well in the wild and no doubt contribute to the overall catch. Wild fish advocates do not want them sharing biological material with true wild stocks, yet they are protected under wild fish prohibitions. In some cases WDFW has imposed mandatory kill regulations on hatchery fish. The irony is that they were stocked by WDFW in the first place, there are limits associated with them, and catch and release is an ethic held by many anglers. How can a conservation agency prohibit catch and release fishing, when, at the same time, there are barbless hook regulations designed specifically to aid in that purpose? (It is crazy!)

Hatchery origin stocks do very well and in fact thrive in local waters, the Great Lakes, New Zealand and particularly in South America. It's not a surprise that WDFW doesn't manage those fish!

One only needs to go salmon fishing at Sekiu in the late summer to see the obvious. Ten to one or even 20 to one caught are often, by definition, wild fish. (Far more than 10 percent are unclipped based upon my observations.) Yet returns of wild fish do not reflect upon those numbers. Largely, for that reason, recreational anglers often distrust the state's numbers.

Assuming a catch and release mortality factor of nearly 20 percent, like the state does, it makes little sense to keep the season open if the unclipped to clipped ratio exceeds five to one. At ten or twenty to one, which is often the case, the fishery often remains open. That is nonsensical if it means an impact to real wild fish. Am I making an argument to close the season sooner? Hell no, I am questioning the assumed mortality rates!

I must once again point out that up to 10 percent of all hatchery coho released, from WDFW hatcheries are intentionally <u>not</u> fin clipped. Of these unmarked fish, many contain coded wire tags. That's why we see fisheries' technicians with hand-held tag recovery wands examining them at hatcheries and at fish buying stations. This statistically based approach is called a *"double blind index"* and useful data is obtained from it. These unclipped, hatchery origin fish remain off limits to anglers and must be released. They are defined as *"<u>wild,</u>"* by WDFW for regulatory purposes. This in spite of the fact that they are <u>provably </u>of hatchery origin. By not making this fact known, WDFW loses much credibility with the courts, not to mention with the angling public.

I must remind the reader that despite the problems that I have with the way hatchery fish being defined by law as being *"wild,"* Officers must remain diligent with enforcing this law from a fair play point of view alone, if not a biological one, because the un-clipped salmon *"may"* be truly wild and therefore deserve protection, and because, if the law abiding angler can't keep the un-clipped fish, no one should.

I am not advocating that anglers cheat with un-clipped fish retention, I merely think the WDFW managers should rethink their management approach.

The basic cornerstone of criminal prosecution is the *"burden of proof."* It is defined as *"reasonable doubt. "* This intentionally very high standard was imposed upon the state, by our founding fathers in order to prevent the innocent from being convicted. WDFW managers neglect to consider this very important standard. They clearly do not consult with their enforcement branch as they should.

The fact that fish, provably of hatchery origin, are protected by regulation, flies in the face of WDFW's stated policy of keeping hatchery fish off the spawning grounds. It makes no sense!

During my last fishing trip to Sekiu, I caught 24 salmon, and only one was a lawful *"clipped"* hatchery fish. Had the daily limit been two salmon, either clipped or unclipped, I would have had a far smaller impact on the 20 plus so called wild salmon that I released. As it was, using the WDFW's own mortality numbers, I killed at least 5 wild fish. Even if ten percent were unclipped hatchery fish, I clearly killed numerous truly wild fish in the process. Had I been allowed to retain *"any"* coho, my total impact on wilds would have been two at the most!

Yes, retaining the first two salmon caught, regardless of if they are clipped or unclipped, in my opinion, would have less impact on truly wild fish. However any useable data from this *"double blind index"* would be rendered null and void.

As it is now, a truly conscientious angler could reasonably believe that he would be saving wild fish by breaking the law.

"How the Department of Fish and Wildlife compel outdoor enthusiasts to cheat." Do you get my title now?

Yes, killing the first two wild fish caught and terminating his trip would be easily rationalized, and the wild fish would be better off, one may think. The only apparent lawful alternative would be not fishing at all, which is exactly what I chose to do on my last day as Sekiu.

Multiply these numbers by thousands, including wild fish impact from other anglers, and you may be as shocked as I. Given the state's reliance on applying encounters as mortalities to cut entire seasons short, I find this approach shocking, and obviously counterproductive.

WDFW also applies a mortality factor called *"drop off"* mortality. Yes, even fish that are not landed, those that "*drop off"* the hook prior to landing or handling of any kind are calculated at a 5% loss. Yet they extend this likelihood by applying boat limits instead of strict individual angler limits for the sole benefit of party boats. (Discussed in the next chapter.)

Is it not certain that millions of unclipped, so called wild salmon, are in fact not wild? Perhaps even millions more that are produced at tribal or federal hatcheries, and intentionally not clipped. (WDFW does it, why shouldn't our co-managers do it too!)

These things are truly unbelievable to me. Especially because WDFW knows all about it. Only a completely detached agency, one with no concept of criminal law, or perhaps one with ulterior motives, would allow it. (WDFW has a fulltime attorney on staff. And a good one at that. WDFW regulators need only ask his opinion.)

"Liberals claim to want to give a hearing to other views, but then are shocked and offended to discover that there are other views." (William F. Buckley Jr.)

8

The insanity continues

Leading the 2021 recreational fishing pamphlet Marine Area Rules section, the following statement is in bold (Page 106);

"In Washington waters where a saltwater license is valid, each angler aboard a vessel may continue to deploy angling gear until the daily limit of fish and shellfish for all anglers aboard has been achieved."

First of all, this regulation was initially approved by a former director of the agency who also operated a salmon fishing charter boat. For him personally, and for many others in that profession, it made sense because it improved the quality of an expensive charter trip. It made the process easier for the boat operator because less time would be spent trying to remember which angler had caught a limit or not, and it would help assure that the entire party retained a limit. Once the angler had done so, prior to this *"director's rule,"* that angler would have to stop fishing for the day. Apparently the law requiring that an angler immediately record his catch on a salmon record card (an easy way to keep track of who caught) what was ignored by charter boats. (Several prior WDFW leaders were at one time high ranking members of the Charter Association.....interesting.)

The effect, was that all paying customers, the skipper and the deckhand, could continue fishing until the collective limit for the group had been retained. Strangely, this law was implemented very quickly. A self-serving conflict of interest perhaps?

Now consider this: As mentioned earlier, a mortality rate regarding fish released has been established. They (WDFW) call it an encounter rate. An arbitrary number anticipating loss was assigned. As stated earlier, this number has a direct effect on how long the season lasts. Seasons are cut short or suspended based upon it. WDFW does so in order to limit the numbers of encounters on wild fish. In fact, WDFW port samplers ask anglers how many encounters they had, in order to assess this unwanted *"take,"* on a daily basis.

Under this regulation, a salmon charter boat, or any boat for that matter fishing in saltwater or the lower Columbia River, can lawfully continue fishing for salmon, albeit without additional salmon retention, until well after the limit of salmon has been retained. This angler trip can only be lawfully terminated after the entire group of paid customers, the crew and the skipper, and / or other licensed anglers aboard, have also retained the collective daily bag limits, for crab, squid, ground fish, mussels, clams, shrimp and arguably even albacore, which don't even have a daily limit! It makes no sense.

This fact greatly increases the number of *"encounters"* with all fish and shortens the season for the rest of us.

All this, in spite of the fact that on page 6 of the regulation pamphlet it says that an angler may not continue to fish after the adult portion of the limit has been retained, **AND**, you may not harvest any part of another person's daily limit! Fish managers that make season closing decisions based on *"encounter rates, and drop offs"* do not consider this fact.

Wouldn't it be better, from an encounter rate point of view, to go back to a two salmon per day limit, period, for all, instead of cutting entire seasons short? The way it is now, anglers must guess correctly upon when they make vacation plans and their lodging reservations. We often forfeit our hard earned cash when the season is suddenly closed.

Don't mind me, I'm just a dumb fish cop.

"Useless laws weaken the necessary laws."(Montesquieu)

Small boat saltwater anglers belong on the endangered species list!

(9)

Possession of frozen herring in Marine Area 12.

Take a look at page 129 of the recreational regulation pamphlet. It very clearly says that it is unlawful to possess herring in Hood Canal. Finally we have a law that is not ambiguous, unfortunately for anglers is makes no sense. Apparently unknown to WDFW, frozen herring is readily available for purchase and it is also a very popular bait for salmon fishing, which is allowed in Hood Canal. It appears that WDFW experts, the ones paid to be aware of such things, are unaware that herring is a popular salmon fishing bait. (Knowledge such as this, apparently does not exist among fish managers.) Also, no one seems to know why herring are unlawful to possess in Hood Canal. Totally absurd regulations such as this, cause me to believe that WDFW is consciously trying, little by little, to phase out recreational fishing.

Note to **WDFW**, Salmon in Hood Canal are known to bite frozen herring. *"The more laws, the more offenders" (Dr. Thomas Fuller)*

10

Bait cures, dyes and other chemicals

On page 8 of the 2021 regulation pamphlet under gear rules it states: *"You may not use drugs explosives or poison that MAY kill or injure fish and wildlife."* This rule, on its surface appears to be sound. I have heard of folks using bleach to extract octopus from their lairs and have personally seen the use of explosives in state waters. (Ironically the explosives were used by a fish and wildlife agency, and many fish died.) Also, WDFW sometimes uses chemicals to kill fish on a large scale. Let's forget for a moment that using a hook, and a net, are known to harm fish. In fact harming the fish, though not necessarily killing it, is the entire point of fishing.

Lead is a real concern and lead sinkers, for obvious reasons, have been restricted in some states.

Again, just for laughs, let's look at some of the ingredients in preserved and processed fishing baits that are used every day by anglers. Better yet take a walk through any fishing gear retail outlet and look at some of the ingredients used. While doing so keep in mind that if it <u>may</u> harm fish, it is unlawful.

These chemicals include:

> ➤ Boric acid (Borax): In powdered form, it is the most common way that anglers cure salmon roe for bait. It is harmful to wildlife and used in pesticide, targeting their stomachs and nervous systems. Also harmful to people if ingested.
> ➤ PVC (Polyvinyl chloride): Common in many popular processed fishing baits and many soft plastic baits,

available at all fishing gear outlets. It contains dangerous chemicals including phthalates, lead and cadmium, which can be toxic to children. (Probably fish). The ever dangerous to fishing in general, Green Peace organization, has ominously declared that some of these ingredients are the biggest threat to aquatic ecosystems. Sport fishing interests should not give them any more ammunition.

➤ Sodium sulfite: Common salmon roe, bait preservative. May be mildly toxic.

Some say that most scented, or soft plastic baits, contain chemicals that may harm fish and or cause fatal intestinal blockages.

➤ Artificial lures (hard plastics) in general contain chemicals that may harm fish. In fact mandatory warning labels (California Proposition 65) are on all similar products. Not to mention that the hooks themselves will harm fish!

➤ Lead head jigs, or a vast array of other lead lures no doubt harm fish and the environment in general. Are they too banned?

Ask yourself, " *Who was the person responsible for suggesting that these products be banned?*" It was almost certainly someone who is not an angler, and perhaps even someone with a hidden *"anti-fishing"* agenda. The good news is that these laws do not exist in an enforceable form...yet. Regardless, it was placed in the recreational fishing pamphlet for a reason (By whom?). Will it be used for yet another attempt by the WDFW Commission to restrict recreational fishing? My fear is that it will!

The very same folks that created the regulatory language regarding bait, at least the ones that go fishing, enthusiastically use all of these products. They remain blissfully ignorant of the possible consequences of what they do and what they write.

I do not believe for a moment that these bait additives pose any significant threat to fish in general, and do not advocate banning them. In fact I use all of them myself. I do however believe that the folks responsible for creating the language used in the regulation publication are woefully ignorant of recreational fishing in general and have no business being in a position to regulate anything. Hell, I don't just believe it, I know it.

Once again, if the enforcement branch of WDFW were consulted regarding this regulatory language, the problem would be easily solved.

"There are so many laws, that no one is safe from hanging."(Napoleon)

11

Closed waters boundaries that do not exist

WDFW holds the fishing public in Washington accountable for many laws. One of the most basic of fishing regulations pertains to fishing area boundary markers. It's important to know where one can fish and where fishing is prohibited!

Unlike other criminal and civil laws, fish and wildlife officers need not prove intent for an angler to be found guilty. They need only to prove that a violation occurred. I believe it's because in theory, the damage is done whether the person knows the law or not. This concept applies to all fish and wildlife criminal violations and civil infractions as well. This legal concept is called *"strict liability."*

There are many areas closed to fishing that are clearly defined and are basically inarguable, such as fishing in a hatchery fish ladder or raceway. Other closed areas are marked by GPS or water depth points of reference, or by specific bodies of water. Some more clearly defined than others. The best fish-don't-fish landmarks are fixed bridges, or geographic points of reference, one would think. However there are many notable exceptions.

On page 125 of the 2021 fishing regulation pamphlet there is a very specific closed waters boundary description in Sinclair Inlet. *"All waters within 150 feet of the pier head line CLOSED to fishing for food fish at all times."*

Strangely, one can fish for game fish, shellfish, or go there for any other reason. You just can't fish for food fish there. I have patrolled that area for more than 30 years, and this regulation has been in effect for nearly all of that time. I have no idea, to what pier they are referencing, nor am I aware what a pier head line is. Furthermore, no one that I know, is aware of what this closure is designed to protect. The pier described, to my knowledge, does not exist.

On page 130 of the same publication a closed area is described near the mouth of Minter Creek. This important marker is in place to protect vulnerable hatchery and wild salmon stocks. Unbelievably, the WDFW decided to use a temporary oyster stake to make this very important distinction. It appears WDFW never considered the inevitable, that the oyster farmer may move this very temporary device. It has not existed for at least 15 years.

Managers know this, and unbelievably, have done nothing but complain to officers about not enforcing the closure at this well-known trouble spot.

Natural cause and effect often changes defined bodies of water that also serve to confuse the angling public. The west fork Satsop River is closed to salmon fishing. The east fork is open. A WDFW boat ramp is located just above the confluence. I launched my boat there this last October and patiently drifted the first several hundred yards of the west fork without making a cast until I entered the open waters of the east fork. This was difficult because I was seeing chrome bright coho the entire time. Fish that would have surely taken my spinner. After reporting the results of my trip to a fish cop friend that evening, I learned that the east fork channel had merged with the west fork a quarter of a mile upstream. What was very recently closed waters were now open! Chalk it up to more forgone opportunity.

Other important distinctions between open and closed areas utilize convenient land marks. One would think that this would be easy, apparently it is not. WDFW makes river mouth definitions that, of course, move and change through natural processes. A futile attempt to fix the problem involved tidal position, but does not adequately address tide level or seasonal tidal change. Even when a fixed bridge is conveniently located where a closed boundary should be, the not so brilliant regulators have decided to use a measured arc from a point at the center of the bridge. They are apparently assuming that all anglers are trained surveyors and have surveying equipment in their tackle box.

The basic concept of what is closed to fishing, and what is open, even when supplied with maps and regulation apps for smart phones, is often a gray area of the law to anglers and fish cops alike. I pity the well-meaning F&W Officer tasked with enforcing these laws, and more so the anglers, whom are expected to comply under penalty of arrest.

Posted signs do not end the debate when contradicted by poor language in the regulation pamphlet. There were many times, as an officer, that I literally drew a line in the sand with the heel of my boot. That worked!

Even in off shore marine areas, where there are no landmarks, fishing is highly restricted. Gone are the days of dead reckoning and triangulating points of reference. The small boat angler, those in perhaps a lower economic class (like me), may not be able to afford expensive navigational gear that is required to stay oriented with the open areas.

Once upon a time, small fiberglass, wooden and aluminum boats, plied all waters of the state seeking ground fish, salmon and halibut far offshore. An entire industry rented boats, small motors and moldy seat cushions. Armed with a small budget, inexpensive rods and a rusty compass, lower income anglers, made wonderful catches. These folks can no longer afford to fish the way we once did. We have been excluded because we don't have enough money. Also, now, fishing depth restrictions are in place requiring expensive sonar.

What's more, these depth restrictions are sometime referenced in fathoms, and sometime in feet. Why not be consistent?

The Wildlife commission is unaware of the history of sport fishing in Washington. Some old photos from the 1960s and 1970s would come as a complete surprise to them.

Once again, if a local F&W officer was consulted regarding the placement of any fishing boundary marker, this chapter would not exist.

"Two types of people laugh at the law: those that break it and those that make it." (Terrence Pratchett)

(12)

The autocrat at work

I am once again going to bring up the same Jerry (not his real name), mentioned in an earlier chapter. This high ranking manager had just been placed into this position with the agency. It was my belief that he being an angler, would be open to a few regulatory suggestions. I organized my thoughts in writing and made my case in his office. It went something like this:

Deschutes Falls Salmon Hatchery gets huge returns of fall chinook every year. The hatchery gets far more fish back that the program needs, therefore thousands of fish are culled, and sold to a fish buyer each fall. In Capitol Lake, just below the hatchery, there was once a very popular chinook fishery that managed to take a few, yet the angler's efforts did not put a dent in the surplus. This fishery is now closed due to an invasive species, the New Zealand Mud Snail, further exasperating the surplus. It appears that the state was worried that kayakers and shore anglers would cause the mud snails to spread. (Other associated bodies infested with the snails are not closed. No one knows why.)

At the foot of the lake is a fish ladder that the fish must pass prior to entering the lake. Huge numbers of chinook gang up just below each fall, and there is not a reason in the world that folks can't fish here. In fact, back in the 1970s the old Department of Fisheries had erected a fishing pier at this site, for disabled anglers. I suggested to Jerry that he once again open the area for fishing.

Jerry said, *"That would cause an enforcement nightmare."* I responded by saying that I was the enforcement there, and that, *"No it wouldn't."* I explained that they are all hatchery fish, and *"there are no wild fish issues. It's an enforcement officer's dream... the fish are surplus, and therefore harvestable!"* I added, *"Why don't we spare them a ride in the cat food truck and let people catch them?"* I explained that it was a ready-made success story. *"No one would object, you would be a hero."* This got his attention.

I was forced to *"dumb down"* my argument to a point where I was uncomfortable. It appeared that this high ranking manager was completely unaware of, or totally indifferent to the fact, that the home stream in question, (Deschutes) is blocked by an impassible water fall. This run of fish is totally artificial. (Green River stock planted in the late 1940's.) The fish are 100 percent of hatchery origin and even a total take, would only serve to enhance wild fish!

I then said that the lower end of the associated saltwater inlet is closed too, and that for identical reasons, there was no reason for the closure. In fact the tribes routinely fish there." "What's more", I advised him, "There *was once a pier at that location set up as a fishing access for disabled anglers. At the very least you can do something like that."*

"I think you're on to something Greg, I'll get back to you."

Of course he didn't. I brought up the subject some time later and he said that he decided not to do it. His only rationale was the *"The Port of Olympia would object to it."* (Any polygraph machine within three miles must have started smoking!)

I was absolutely floored once again! It is the Washington Department of Fish and Wildlife's mission to preserve, protect, and to promote recreational opportunity! Opening this area would be a ready-made success story. The angling public and others would applaud it. The tribes would not object either. Anglers have already paid for the opportunity to catch these fish, they have suffered other cutbacks and deserve a break!

Sadly, this high ranking administrator, in a position to do something productive and who could affect an opening with a stroke of a pen, was blaming his inaction on the Port of Olympia!

I later made an enquiry at the port and no one knew what I was talking about. No one at the Port Of Olympia was opposed to the idea of opening the fishery.

"Why should we be? We don't manage salmon."

That folks, is a classic example of what we are up against!

"We are all born ignorant, but one must work hard to remain stupid." (Benjamin Franklin)

Another fishing license ambiguity

There are many definitions on page 18 of the 2021 regulation pamphlet that makes no sense. In fact many do not appear any place else in the publication, and are useless to the angling consumer. Let's look at one in particular. Keep in mind that the angler, when deciding whether he wants to purchase a saltwater or freshwater license (valid only for the venue chosen, or both, at a higher cost), must make a decision. If he or she chooses wrongly, he or she is subject to a criminal charge and all of the trappings, to include arrest, forfeiture of equipment and / or citation. And yes, such action would appear on a rudimentary background check, and could threaten a person's employment.

- **Freshwater Area:** *Those waters within any freshwater river, lake, stream or pond. On the bank or within 10 yards of any lake river or pond.* ***On ANY boat launch, ramp, or parking facility associated with ANY freshwater, river, lake or pond.***

This definition makes no sense, and does not support any other regulation that I know. I am at a total loss to understand what purpose it serves.

How can a parking lot or dry land be defined as fresh water? It doesn't say this applies only to WDFW facilities, but any boat ramp! But most of all, I know of many boat ramps, both public and private, that are associated with freshwater bodies that are solidly within saltwater, and in fact have a thick layer of marine organisms clinging to them!

The question remains: Do I buy a fresh water license to fish here, or a saltwater license? Well, he or she better buy both even though it's far more expensive. Is this an intentional trap? Or does it reflect the sloppy work of a cubicle bound administrator? How is it that WDFW remains unaware of such things. Does it take an obsessed, retired officer to point this, and many other nonsensical regulations, out? Regardless, any prudent enforcement officer would have to accept either license, if aware of this definition.

More realistically, this definition diminishes the ability of officers to enforce any license requirement!

Here is one more point about fishing licenses. If an angler moved to the state of Washington and qualified for residency in the month of January, he would go the the local license vender and purchase a fishing license for that calender year, then go fishing. Little does he know that his license is not valid untill April.

If this potential angler had the where-with-all to have asked for a license showing the previous year, not a logical choice on its face because its not the same year anymore, that license would expire in April! Could he get a ticket through no fault if his own? Yes he could.

Once again, this would be an easy fix, if enforcement professionals were consulted.

"Lex malla, lex nulla." (Bad law, no law.) St. Thomas Aquinas, 1274.

Frustrated anglers making a point.

(14)

More Hypocrisy

The following example is not totally the fault of the WDFW, other than they could have stopped it at the time it was imposed or, they could, and they should, enforce it now.

WDFW is so incompetent about establishing effective laws that private citizens and anti-hunting activist groups often seize upon the opportunity to do it for them.

Several initiatives, backed by a popular vote, and supported largely by non-hunters or anti hunters, have become law on my watch. Bear baiting was outlawed, as was the hunting with hounds for a number of species. In addition, body gripping traps were prohibited. Each of these initiatives greatly inhibited hunting opportunity. This in spite of WDFW's mission statement: *"To promote recreational opportunities."*

When Lewis and Clark came west back in 1804 they were interested in establishing a trade route from the mouth of the Columbia River to points in the east. It was not gold they were seeking, but they no doubt examined mineral deposits along the way. It was not timber, nor fish, or any of the things that you may think. No it was not a place to build aircraft or rivers to dam, that all came later.

What they sought was a way to transport furs from the Pacific Northwest. Although insignificant now, at the time, furs may as well have been gold. A trapping culture was established and it lasted well into the 20th century. Even now, folks augment their household income by trapping. Their problem is they can no longer use body gripping traps. (One exception are traditional rat and mouse traps, but rat hides are not worth much.)

The anti-body gripping trap laws were poorly thought out. No consideration went to the folk trying to keep their family traditions alive or to those attempting to augment their often meager income. (Poor folk are very vulnerable these days.)

WDFW contracts hound hunters to capture bears, often with lethal intent. Ditto, problem cougars. They allow private timber companies to bait and lethally control bear populations with hounds. They recognize that baiting and hunting with hounds are the only effective way to control their populations. Yet for a citizen to do so is potentially a felony level crime with a mandatory license suspension. WDFW biologists actively snare bears as well. Enforcement officers routinely use hounds and baited live traps. I truly do not understand how WDFW can get away with this hypocrisy.

 And what really pisses me off is that the Wildlife Code now prohibits the trapping of moles! In fact, I know of several cases where people were charged criminally with mole trapping, in an attempt to keep their lawn looking nice!

If an elk was eating your crops, or a bear causing damage or even if deer are eating your roses, you can apply for a permit and shoot the offenders. An officer is authorized to approve this even without a formal permit in hand. But a mole damaging your lawn, forget it. Ironically, one IS allowed to shoot moles. You can gas them, smash them with a shovel, spear them with a stick. You can blow them up, set them on fire or sic your dog on them. But the only effective and humane way to do it is with a body gripping trap, and that is prohibited by the game code. Yes, you can go to jail, pay a fine, have your property seized **AND** have your license suspended for trapping a mole with a body gripping trap. There are other things to consider as well.

A body gripping trap is defined as:

(2) "Body gripping trap" means a trap that grips an animal's body or body part. (Includes snares and yes, fish are defined by law as "Animals.")

RCW 77.15.194 (1) "Animal" means any non-human vertebrate.

In the meantime, WDFW allows the use of gill nets on a very large scale. Gillnets are designed to entangle, ensnare and to grip fish and their body parts.

This is a clear contradiction, ignored by WDFW. In my opinion, gillnet fisheries are in violation of this law.

The body gripping trap prohibition is a bad law! I submit to the reader that if you're going to ignore one obvious application of it, in the interest of fairness, you must ignore the other as well. Again WDFW loses credibility with the courts, or at least the enforcement officers do, yet the officers had nothing to do with creating this ambiguity.

It must be nice (and convenient) to enforce some laws and to totally ignore others.

"Dying societies accumulate laws like dying men accumulate remedies" (Nicolas Gomez Davila)

A criminal mole trapper at large, she will never talk.

(15)

Northern Pike Minnow Bounty System

BPA, otherwise known and the Bonneville Power Administration, is heavily involved in salmon mitigation projects largely focused upon the Columbia River. They finance a well-intended project, conducted by the Washington State Department of Fish and Wildlife that seeks to reduce the numbers of Northern Pike Minnow from a section of the Columbia River. Known to feed on salmon, particularly juvenile chinook, this native species is caught and killed by anglers by the thousands in exchange for a cash reward put up by **BPA**.

Let me be clear, the target of the bounty program is a native species that have harmoniously coexisted with pacific salmon for thousands of years. In the meantime, smallmouth and largemouth bass, and walleye, all highly abundant **NON NATIVE** fish that were introduced largely by unlawful means. They highly protected by slot limits, size, bag, license and sometime seasonal limitations. All of these non-natives, prey heavily on juvenile salmon, but it's the native species that demands a cash reward upon its death! The non-natives, invasive in my book, remain protected by strict regulation.

It's possible that the Pike Minnow bounty program may someday stress the population to the point of listing it under the Endangered Species Act. (How would WDFW explain that colossal blunder?) Historically, cash bounties on wolves, grizzly bears, and other animals, have had that affect.

To impose a cash bounty in the year 2022 on a **NATIVE** species, poorly reflects a so-called conservation agency that is unaware of history, and has total ignorance of biological control strategies in general. This is an agency whose managers seem to pride themselves in getting such species listed under the Endangered Species Act. This strategy appears to be reckless.

Did I mention that if the same encounter rates that apply to salmon in saltwater areas were applied to the many juvenile salmon caught and killed due to this program, WDFW would cancel this program in a New York minute!

To my knowledge there has been no measureable increase in adult chinook returns due to the Northern Pike Minnow bounty program. It continues to this day.

I am deeply ashamed of the agency that I worked for, for thirty nine years.

"Wildlife, cash bounty programs, have always failed in one way or another. For a modern conservation agency to impose one on a native species, while protecting non-natives with strict regulation, defies logic, and demonstrates an anachronistic application of wildlife management strategies" (Author quote)

(16)

More errors and conflicting language in the current recreational fishing regulations (2022)

Be aware that many of the individual points made in the following chapter are contradicted in other locations of the regulation pamphlet. This fact compounds its collective ambiguity.

For an old fish cop, looking through the current regulation pamphlet is a frustrating experience. He or she recognizes things that did not make sense thirty years ago, mixed in with additional tidbits that make no sense or are completely false now.

 Any administrator that defends this regulatory system, is either completely out of touch with reality or a fool. I cannot turn a page of this 150 page collection of bird cage liner, and not laugh, or sometimes cry out loud. Each page, and many times each column, brings out in me words and or a reaction that I cannot appropriately express here.

To think that I actually used this publication to enact due process of law, train new officers, or educate the public, now causes me great conflict.

Let's take a look at only a few statewide fresh water rules.

> ➤ Fresh water areas are open 24 hours per day when open.

False: *Many freshwater areas have night restrictions.*

➢ Hook and line angling only.

False: *Carp may be taken by bow and arrow. Spear fishing is allowed in some areas, as are cast nets and dip nets.*

➢ It is unlawful to take fish taken from fresh water that was not hooked in the mouth or on the head.

False: *Smelt / forage fish may be jigged. Carp may be bow hunted.*

➢ (2) It is unlawful for any person to take, fish for, or possess fish taken for personal use by any means other than angling with a line attached to a pole held in hand while landing the fish or with a hand-operated line without rod or reel, except:
  (a) It is unlawful to fish for or possess salmon taken for personal use with hand lines in marine waters of Puget Sound east of the mouth of the Sekiu River and in Washington waters at the mouth of the Columbia River east of a line projected true north and south through Buoy 10
  (b) Grays Harbor, and Willapa Bay.

Unlawful to use hand lines in some areas but not others? Apparently we have a major problem with folks using hand lines! Glaring errors like this, individually don't mean much, but they add up to weaken the effectiveness of all WDFW laws. Not a big deal but does anyone know why? This law has been in effect for many years.

➢ Possession of game fish is two daily limits in any form.

False: *You may purchase rainbow trout, channel catfish or other cultured species of game fish in any amount.*

➢ WAC 220.20...(2) "Anti-snagging rule" means: (a) Except when fishing with a buoyant lure (with no weights added to the lure or line) or trolling from a vessel or floating device, terminal fishing gear is limited to a lure or bait with one single point hook. (b) Only single point hooks measuring not more then 3/4 inch from point to shank may be used and all hooks must be attached to or below the lure or bait.

Anti-snagging rules. Once again there is a clear bias against lower income, shore bound anglers. The bank angler is far more limited in his or her movements than the boat angler already, and therefore more negativity affected by this rule.

➢ Crappie (and others) No minimum size /no daily limit.

False: *There are minimums and bag limits on crappie in some areas.*

➤ Salmon: Anglers may not continue to fish for salmon after the adult portion of the limit has been retained.

Absurd: *Most freshwater salmon seasons allow for the retention of up to 6 jack salmon. Also, this is not true in salt water.*

➤ Grass Carp Closed.

Absurd... Who cares?

➤ Salmon / game fish possession limits.

If lawfully caught / possessed, why is there a possession limit?

➤ Some fish may only be used for human consumption or bait.

Again if lawfully possessed, it's not the state's business how they are utilized.

➤ Release all wild steelhead.

False: May be retained on many Indian reservations and transported off reservation. Unclipped rainbow trout, over 20 inches in length (indistinguishable from steelhead) may be retained in the upper Columbia River or nearly any place else for that matter. If chopped up at the fishing site, and transported back to the car on foot, no one will ever know!

➢ Why are herring, sand lance and anchovies listed under freshwater rules?

No one knows!

➢ You may not possess Dolly Varden- Bull Trout in the field in such a condition that the species and total length cannot be determined.

Think about this, if you cannot determine the species, I guess its okay to possess the Bull Trout. (Who writes this stuff?) On the very next page, there is an allowance for possessing Bull Trout. One can possess them if caught in a gill net and sold by a tribal member!

➢ *You may not snag or attempt to snag fish.*

False: Forage fish may be snagged. Inadvertent snagging in fresh water is not a crime. Inadvertently snagged fish in marine areas may be retained if the season is open.

For 45 years the Department permitted the La Conner Smelt Derby. Surf smelt were targeted by snagging. The sponsors paid cash and issued prizes to paying participants. All with the total knowledge of, and approval of the department despite their own published regulations.

Salmon may be snagged, if done so inadvertently. A very common occurrence in rivers where fishing is open. Only when the fish is intentionally foul hooked, or if a snagged fish is retained, is there a violation. Not so in salt water, where a snagged salmon, or any other food fish may be retained, if open to fishing.

> ➤ You may not use drugs, explosives or poisons that may harm fish.

Ha, I already wrote a chapter about that!

> ➤ Possession limits: In marine areas 1-6, anglers on board a boat may only possess one daily limit of fish or shellfish. Salmon, halibut steelhead and bottom fish, tuna and shellfish.

Why is it different in other marine areas? Why are they not the same? Is it because the salmon, steelhead, halibut bottom fish, tuna and shellfish regulator can't communicate with his colleagues?

> ➤ You may not use any type of chemical irritant to harvest fish unless a special exemption has been made by the director.

It's nice to know people in high places! Why is this in the recreational pamphlet? To my knowledge this has never been done!

➢ All Fishing Gear (In bold) must be kept in immediate control, and gear may not be left unattended while fishing.

False: Crab gear, shrimp gear, crayfish gear, etc. may be unattended, for days at a time! Also, it appears that one can get a ticket for a bathroom break with your rod in a holder!

➢ Descending gear must be on board while fishing for or in possession of halibut or bottom fish.

True, but incredibly, an angler is not required to use it!

➢ Special rules (Bold, and in red): Salmon, single point barbless hooks and a hand held rod must be used.

False: Two rods may be used in marine area 13, landlocked salmon in lakes are regulated as trout and barbed hooks are allowed.

➢ Salmon are classified as game fish in some bodies of water and as food fish in others.

My god, who writes this stuff.

➤ Some fish are measured in fork length, others are measured by total length.

Why? Just to be as confusing as possible?

➤ In Puget Sound, only chinook salmon have a size limit. Coho, Chum, Sockeye and Pinks do not... *Why?*

No one knows!

➤ One can use up to 9 barbed hooks if fishing with forage fish jig gear in marine areas.

Don't the managers know that any attempt to catch forage fish this way results in the unintended take of many juvenile salmon? Apparently none have ever done it. Also this gear is commonly used to fish by pier bound anglers targeting shiner perch. They are all crooks I guess.

➤ Page 6 column 2: You may not transport live fish...without a permit.

What are they saying here? How does one use live forage fish for bait without somehow transporting it? Are they saying I can't transport live clams, fish, crab or shrimp in a bucket? What about the bass angler and his $50,000 bass boat or the charter boat rigged with a live tank? Are they crooks too? Next *time you go the pet store to replace your kid's dead goldfish, you better get a permit first! Unbelievable!*

> ➢ In many freshwater bodies of water, jack salmon accompany "adult" salmon. "Jacks" are defined by size. Chinook between 12 and 24 inches are regulated as *"jacks." "Adults"* are defined by those over 24 inches. The reality is that jacks are in fact adult fish and are totally capable of spawning in the wild and in a hatchery setting. "The term *"adult"* to separate "jacks" is misleading.

A typical freshwater regulation will allow for the take of six salmon, no more than two may be adult salmon. But at the same time, once the adult portion of the limit is retained, the angler is, by regulation, done fishing for the day. Yet if he or she catches his jacks first, he can continue fishing until the 6 fish limit is retained.

In the meantime, particularly where fishing is good, the angler "encounters" numerous other fish that do not fit the criteria allowed by his daily limit. Although released, each encounter is considered an impact by WDFW that accounts for a calculated number of dead fish.

Not only is WDFW dictating the order in which an angler catches his fish, totally absurd in my mind, they are also inadvertently and unnecessarily increasing the number of encounters. Yet they do all they can to limit the number of encounters in other areas, including closing the season! Just pick a reasonable number and print it. It's simple!

Just in case you see it, buried in the fine print, the WDFW thinks it's important to distribute over 100,000 regulation pamphlets that point out:

> ➤ *If 6 or more game fish anglers, over 15 years old, decide to have a friendly contest regarding who catches the biggest fish, a fishing contest permit is required. (Page 15) If only five friends so compete, no permit is required.*

"If I didn't know any better I would say that the regulators are all on drugs." (Author quote)

Puget Sound and coastal rivers

I don't have the patience to provide a complete analysis of this section of the recreational pamphlet. One quick glance will leave the average recreational fisherman shaking his head.

➢ The Bogachiel River alone has 10 different opening and closing dates that an angler must keep track of. In addition, it has 12 different *"additional special rules."* Not listed, is an emergency closure of all steelhead fishing for the remainder of 2022.

➢ A fairly small tributary of this river, the Calawah River, has fifteen dates to remember and an additional twenty additional special rules. Again, not listed, is the current all steelhead closure.

➢ The Chehalis River, lists 24 separate dates regarding fishing openings and closures and 27 special rules. Twenty nine dates are to be memorized by fish cops and anglers for the Green River, with 31 additional special rules. The Naselle River, 42 dates and 46 respectively. I can go on and on. You are starting to get my point!

➢ The far less significant, Forks Creek in Pacific County, one with no wild fish issues that I am aware of, shows 9 dates, and 11 additional special rules.

➢ Two hundred and twenty six streams are listed in this section all with equally confusing dates and special rules. Consider for a moment that **statewide general rules** add significantly to these ambiguities.

> Some freshwater areas have "stationary gear rules" in place, which appear to criminalize an angler who accidently snags up his gear!

WAC 220-300-160

Definitions—Personal-use fishing (30) "Stationary gear restriction" means the line and weight and lure or bait must be moving while in the water. The line and weight and lure or bait may not be stationary.

> Shellfish license not required for three species of non-native shellfish. (Red Swamp, Rusty, and Northern crayfish.)

An entire page and 4 color photos are dedicated to identifying these species. In 39 years with WDFW, I never saw anyone fishing for them. The irony is that licenses <u>are</u> required to fish for numerous other non-native shellfish. (Japanese oysters, Manilla clams, Varnish clams and Invasive Green crabs.)

> On pages 27, 28 and 101 of the recreational fishing pamphlet there are color photos of 16 game fish species that occur in Washington.

Presumably, these pictures are there to assist the angler with identification. All but two are <u>non-native</u> and do not belong in Washington. Numerous species of common <u>native</u> game fish species are not depicted at all (burbot, mountain whitefish, pike minnow, etc.) What does this say about WDFW's conservation priorities?

> On page one, paragraph one, the current fishing regulation pamphlet, unambiguously states:

"This pamphlet is a summary of fishing regulations..... This pamphlet does not contain nor is it intended to contain all department regulations." (Are they saying there's more?)

To top it all off, the WDFW also imposes hundreds of emergency rules which often go into effect in a matter of mere hours after an on line notice. Very often, these sudden changes are flawed and / or poorly worded, much to the frustration of enforcement officers and anglers. Often they are season ending announcements that lack justification. In at least one recent case the season was closed because WDFW forgot to renegotiate an ESA permit with the Feds. Some emergency closures are the result of written complaints addressed to just the right person.

They are promulgated under the authority of:

RCW 34.05.350

Emergency rules and amendments.(1) If an agency for good cause finds:

> (a) That immediate adoption, amendment, or repeal of a rule is necessary for the preservation of the public health, safety, or general welfare, and that observing the time requirements of notice and opportunity to comment upon adoption of a permanent rule would be contrary to the public interest;

The disturbing thing about this annoying habit, is that oftentimes fishing regulations are changed without a true emergency. Furthermore, anyone empowered by the director can impose such rules without legislation or even without a true consensus.

"So, no matter how good a student of the regulations an angler may be, no matter how conscientious, or astute with the law, or even an enforcement officer of the agency, he or she can never be totally sure what the fishing regulations are on any given day. Tell that to the guy in line to buy his license! This is the sad truth." (Author quote)

Welcome to fishing in Washington, we hope you enjoy your angling experience. Come back when we get this crap figured out!

"If a man can't remember the laws, then he's got too many of them" (Richard Dawkins)

Most anglers are more than happy to release a wild fish.

18

Who to blame?

It would be very interesting to put the responsible person's name to each of the unnecessary, ambiguous and totally false do's and don'ts printed within the regulation pamphlet. (Maybe I'll do that next.) Many of the most confusing regulations can be easily traced to a mere handful of managers.

Yet few of them have been around long enough to know that many regulatory points currently in print, were originally created for reasons that no longer exist, and perhaps never did.

Just last fall the daily limit of hatchery coho in marine area 13 was reduced to one fish despite agency assurances of a healthy return. It takes a dumb fish cop to know that in extreme south Puget Sound there are no streams with established wild coho escapement goals. The sometimes abundant fish, that return here are raised and released from net pens and don't even have a stream to call their own.

Why, pray tell, was the limit reduced, then mysteriously bumped back to two fish right after they stopped biting. Or was it because WDFW negligently allowed their federal permit, that kept the season open, to expire?

There may be legitimate explanations to these questionable decisions. Let's hear them. Transparency would go a long way towards improving my attitude.

Clearly, these guys, the regulators that is, are not anglers and have not tried to abide by their own regulations. Once again, they are truly hopeless.

Does the WDFW Wildlife Commission assign oversight to the regulatory process? One would think that would be their appointed director. Clearly he does not do it. Is it the fish program? Well, apparently not. What about the regional directors who represent the director on a regional level. Well, no one seems to know what those folks are supposed to do. (In fact, it has come to my attention that they often delegate their law changing authority to subordinates, when out of the office. If they ever left me in charge, even for a minute, I could have done some good.)

 That leaves the biologists and project managers to blame. Presumably, the ones that apply " *The best available science*" after studying things, collecting data and passing this information on up the chain. Notably absent on this list, those not to blame, are the professional law enforcement officers. Yet they are the only ones that understand how laws should be applied, yet ironically, the ones that get the blame.

 All of these pieces should be linked like a chain, instead they are tumbling around a cyberspace cloud.

"Creating unenforceable laws, to fill the gaps in scientific knowledge, is typical of the WDFW." (Author quote)

19

Unfortunate truth

Remember that a Fish and Wildlife police officer is also tasked with enforcing laws under totally different RCWs. They are a primary enforcer of boating safety laws, sanitary shellfish and ATV (all-terrain vehicle) compliance.

Enforcing boating safety laws are often perceived as a clandestine search for fishing violations and vice versa. It isn't and never should be. Officers utilize their enforcement discretion far more often that is widely believed by the angling public.

As anyone with common sense can see, pointing out errors in the current (as of this writing) recreational fishing rules pamphlet, is child's play. This is much like beating a dead horse.

Since fish and wildlife violations tend to be thought of as minor crimes by many courts, prosecutors and judges included, they do not interest the best prosecutors and or defense attorneys. When a really bright, aggressive prosecutor takes an interest in fish and wildlife cases, it's been my experience that they soon move up the ladder to the superior court level where recreational cases are generally not heard.

True in most applications of criminal law, defendants in fish and wildlife cases, tend to come from a much lower socio economic class. Yes that means poor people.

These folks are almost inevitably assigned a public defender at public cost. They tend to cut plea deals and prosecutors are more than happy to accommodate them. For this reason, fish and wildlife cases tend to not go to trial, but are resolved through negotiations, where both sides give and take. Often a resolution is reached.

In my opinion, if there was real money involved, the F. Lee Baileys and Johnny Cochrans of the world would get fish and wildlife charges dismissed with a quiet fart. The quality of work put forward by the officers in the field is not the problem, this is due to the low quality of work put forward by those who write the regulations.

I believe that fish and wildlife crimes, and the regulations currently in place, exploit the poor, and especially, non-English speaking groups. Let's face it, being able to read the English language doesn't help me understand the nonsense contained within the current recreational regulations.

Am I calling the manufacturers of fish and wildlife regulations racist? Well, I hope this suggestion gets their attention. Being called a racist is the biggest nightmare for liberal and progressive thinking individuals. They certainly spend a lot of time calling police officers racist, but usually only when enforcing laws they created!

As things are today, enforcement officers apply an immense amount of discretion while making their *"cite don't cite"* decisions, as they should. It's to the point where violations that should result in a citation are often dealt with by a warning. Officers are very aware of the printed flaws in the regulation pamphlet. Nonetheless, it's the field officer that takes the heat, and at times the abuse from the public, when the persons actually responsible remain insulated from it.

"Poverty is like punishment for a crime you didn't commit."
(Eli Khamarov)

(20)

The problems with game regulations

Recreational hunting laws are, for the most part, far more understandable than those of recreational fishing. The reason for this is most likely that game management models are far simpler.

Relatively few game animals are listed as threatened under the Endangered Species Act. There is relatively little inadvertent take of those that are listed as such. ESA listed salmon die every day for man-made causes, but if a grizzly bear, wolf , lynx or wolverine gets killed, its front page news.

For once I will make a point in defense of the fish manager. Their issues are clearly far more complex. Marine fish and migratory fish in general, are less limited by geography in their movements, therefore harmful impacts are more diverse and therefore more likely. Those of game animals are far more controllable.

Another reason that game regulations make more sense is that clearly it's a different, less competitive, and more sensible group of folks that make them. I believe that folks in WDFW's wildlife program tend to be conscientious hunters as well as managers. They tend to see the regulations in terms of real life. Fish managers tend not to, but I will admit that the fish managers' job is more complex. That is all I can say in their defense.

What I do see happening with hunting regulations is that when new rules are imposed, they often make some sense and are arguably justified, but just as often they have unintended consequences!

However, much of the language contained within the Big Game hunting regulation pamphlet remains ambiguous.

Hunting is defined as: *"Any attempt to kill, capture, injure, or harass a wild animal or wild bird."* I guess that means chasing a raccoon off ones porch with a broom requires a hunting license!

"Oh, the unintended consequences of perfidy." (Andrew Levkoff)

Read on.

21

Road kill salvage laws

A few years back, consistent with numerous other states, WDFW decided to allow for the salvage of road kill deer and elk. I liked the idea, at first. A large portion of my patrol time and call outs were responding to car/deer accidents.

Other police agencies were reluctant to shoot injured deer because often a complex report regarding the discharge of a weapon was required. Not so with us.

I killed many deer and elk over the years when they needed to be put down. And it was a shame that the meat was not utilized as it should have been.

Although, I feel compelled to admit, that I was known to look the other way from time to time, and developed an *"I don't care what happens to the carcass"* attitude. As did many other, mostly *"old school carcass cops."*

Currently, if there is a dead deer or elk on the side of the road a person may pick it up and salvage it. He or she must purchase a $10 permit within 24 hours in order to document the animal. Regulatory follow-up to this requirement is minimal. There is no limit to the number of animals so salvaged.

It appears to be a great rule and reflects some degree of thought but it's not without unintended fallout.

Now, imagine that you are the Game Warden. You get a frantic call from a reliable informant. He tells you that there is a pickup truck traveling southbound on Interstate Five with ten dead deer and an elk in plain view. It is March and all hunting seasons are closed. The vehicle appears in front of you and you confirm the report with your own eyes.

Since there is no limit on salvaged deer or elk, and your informant provided no information to suggest that the animals were unlawfully taken or possessed an officer must take pause. There is still action that a Game Warden can take but his or her task becomes far more difficult.

Given this scenario, what you can do is very limited. Prior to the road kill salvage law, this was not the case. Furthermore, any report of suspected unlawful deer or elk in a residence, without probable cause that the animals were unlawfully taken, (To be determined by a judge) is far less usable than it was prior to the road kill salvage law. Yes, a law intended to make the Game Wardens job easier, has had the opposite result.

A few years back, I discovered a disturbing trend. Over the course of a few weeks I noticed piles of apples and produce spread out on several rural roadways.

One day I noticed a freshly killed deer laying near one of the piles. I continued my patrol. Several hours later, I noticed that the pile of produce had been refreshed and the dead deer was gone. In a rush, it dawned on me that someone taking advantage of this seemingly good law was setting up baits to get deer killed, with no consideration to the safety of motorists.

I advised many other officers of what I had seen. Some also reported piles of apples and other produce placed at suspicious locations.

I retired shortly thereafter but as of this writing I still wonder about the overall extent of this kind of activity. I looked into it at the time and discovered several addresses within about a five mile radius that had applied for road kill salvage permits. I was stymied because the system used to record and contain this data did not hold up to law enforcement standards, so any information held within the system was not useable.

It appears that we have yet one more new law with an unknown amount of abuse potential, as well as one more that limits the effectiveness of law enforcement efforts.

"Most of the mistakes in thinking are inadequacies of perception rather than mistakes of logic" (Edward de Bono)

22

Can one hunt from a car or not?

For many years it was unlawful to possess a loaded long gun in a motor driven vehicle. Folks were constantly asking if they could take a rest across the hood of the car, or from a pickup truck bed, while shooting a deer. Someone, not an enforcement officer, decided that doing so made sense, despite the fact that it remains unlawful to hunt from a vehicle.

The language of the law was changed to allow for using the frame of a vehicle, or hood, for a shooting rest. Shortly thereafter I had the following experience:

While driving down a rural roadway during modern elk season, traffic ahead of me was stopped. I observed a man wearing hunter orange, standing in the back of a pickup, parked with the engine running in the middle of the road. He was aiming a scoped rifle at a bull elk and using a kid's shoulder as a shooting rest. He fired, and the elk went down.

I processed what I believed to be numerous violations of the game code. Including: Loaded long gun in motor driven vehicle, unlawfully shoot to, from, along or across a publically maintained road, and hunt with a motor vehicle.

Later, while discussing the case with a prosecutor he advised me that the language had changed regarding the shooting from a vehicle law. Although you could not shoot from *"in"* the vehicle, one could shoot from *"on"* the vehicle. In the bed of the pickup, was in his opinion, "on" the vehicle.

Furthermore one can now possess a loaded long gun *"on"* the vehicle, but not *"in"* the vehicle. I also learned that one <u>can</u> shoot too from or across a publically maintained roadway IF one does not do it *"negligently."* In this case there was a dirt back stop and the bullet went directly through an elk's heart. I could not articulate *"negligence."* In this case, one word, *"on"* was added and *"in"* was dropped. This made several previously unlawful acts lawful.

This is a perfect example of an unintended consequence of fixing a law that was not broken. If an officer was consulted prior, it would not have happened.

"A great many people think they are thinking when they are merely rearranging their prejudices." (William James)

Shoot from the road? I guess there's no problem.

(23)

Hunt while trespass law

This law was created and pushed by the Enforcement Program in 2012, I believe. I blame this bone head move on an out of touch Chief who was no advocate of sportsmen.

This law too, had unintended consequences, easily anticipated in my opinion. Before this law went into effect, criminal trespass in the second degree was already a crime. The problem was that if a hunter trespassed onto an area designated as privately owned *"walk in hunting only,"* the only lawful remedy was to charge second degree trespass under RCW 9.A. Although criminal by definition, this law did not allow for the seizure of elk or deer so taken, nor for the forfeiture of associated equipment, like the wildlife code allows. (RCW 77) Those in power at the time wanted to be able to seize property!

Previous to this law on numerous occasions, I contacted trespassing hunters with game in possession. I would charge the crime of second degree criminal trespass but had to let the violators retain the spoils. In addition, although clearly an unlawful act, I could not forfeit rifles or associated equipment. The problem was that any fine imposed for this charge would be deferred or be very minimal. Simply stated, it was often well worth it for folks to trespass while hunting.

This law passed with virtually no opposition. The creators of this law failed to think it through.

Now it is a violation of the game code <u>and</u> title 9.A to do so. Seizure of unlawfully taken wildlife and equipment used, while trespassing is now the norm.

The new law has some vagueness to it, inevitable in my opinion when legislators get ahold of things, but once again the unintended consequence was huge.

This law was the catalyst for industrial timberland owners to charge hunters for access. A law guaranteed to help their interests by creating a new revenue source. By charging people to access their lands, it also guaranteed a private police force to enforce it. (No other law enforcement agency wants to enforce the game code for all the aforementioned reasons.)

In the meantime, WDFW liberally approves bear depredation kill permits to prevent timber damage, when timber companies could allow additional hunter access to control the bear population.

I often express the mantra that the WDFW mission statement is to promote recreational opportunity. In this case, hunting opportunity was inadvertently, yet severely, curtailed.

Another thing that I find very disturbing is that the number of deer lawfully harvested in western Washington, prior to this law going into effect, has been cut by about half. Overall harvest remains lower, the black tail deer population is rising, yet no mechanism for increased harvest has been imposed in public areas, even though black tail deer populations and common sense support the idea. At the same time, bear hunting opportunity was similarly restricted, and ultimately decreased even on public grounds with no biological justification.

I believe that the current Wildlife Commission is consciously using these facts to phase out big game hunting in general. I can make a strong circumstantial case to support this assertion. Although called *"fear mongering"* by current commissioners, this concept has been proven by the recent commission action eliminating the annual spring bear hunt, which was biologically not justified.(And other things.)

No, I do not like this new law, especially when a permit to access industrial timberlands costs $500 or more. Once again, folks that cannot afford it must find more populated areas to hunt. Public areas are overcrowded. Hunting is not only less safe, but less productive. Deer, elk and bear that otherwise could be harvested are not. Yet bear depredation permits are issued by WDFW to the timber companies by the hundreds.

Low cost food and recreational opportunity is denied to hunters in lower economic classes and many hunters decide to spend what money they have, hunting out of state, or in urban areas, where conflicts with anti-hunters are inevitable.

Yes, lower income hunters have an incentive to violate hunting regulations as they currently exist.

All of this was made possible by one person who failed to recognize the inevitable, by being totally unaware of how this law would further restrict hunting opportunity. Nor was he aware that such a law would create a clear conflict of interest for the agency.

"Government despotism is never so fierce and so powerful as when it rests on the fictitious popular will." (Mikhail Bakunin)

(24)

Proof of sex or species must remain naturally attached

If a hunter successfully kills a big game animal or a game bird, proof of sex, or of the species (game birds) must remain naturally attached to the animal while in the field.

Let's say an elk hunter kills a bull elk 12 miles from any road. He or she must field dress the animal in such a way that proof of sex remains naturally attached. This means that the genitals, or parts of them, remain on one of the quarters. This makes packing out the animal, always in pieces, problematic but not impossible. However, since the burden of proof, regarding proof of sex falls upon the state, and that proof of sex remains in every cell of the bull elk's body, it seems to me that this requirement should not be placed upon the hunter, but upon the state.

The same is true with game birds where an un-plucked wing must remain naturally attached while in transport. This aids the officer with identification and keeping with daily limits. Once again, proof of species remains in every cell in the bird's body, yet the burden of proof is placed upon the hunter, not the state. I see these requirements as unconstitutional, or at least vague.

This point may seem nit-picky with many hunters, but only because they are all too accustomed to excessive scrutiny. Yet the burden of proof regarding crimes, remain with the state, in all other aspects of criminal law.

Again, little things such as this, add up to diminish the credibility of all wildlife regulations.

Three point minimum requirements for elk depends upon an antler fork in relation to the natural position of the ear. I have many times joined officers busily manipulating a dead elk's ear, alongside the fork of an antler, even though the antler clearly had three antler points! *"What position was the ear in when the hunter fired his rifle? We will never know, so the animal is lawful!"*

This is an example of a well-meaning, but unrealistic game biologist making laws without the perspective of a fair thinking enforcement officer.

There seems to be no oversight to recreational hunting regulations either.

"When a liberal scientist makes a new law, it is done so without thought to enforceability, or solid legal foundation. Due process of law, the constitution and common sense are not considered." (Author quote)

(25)

Game Wastage laws

It is unlawful for the edible portions of game animals to be *"recklessly"* wasted. Once again, on the surface this law appears to make sense. However, I hate liver. My family hates liver. I also can't stand the idea of eating tripe, kidneys, deer fat, hoofs, cartilage or brain. I throw it all away! On the other hand, I keep the hide, and carefully harvest the sinew for my other hobby that includes securing primitive arrow points, made from bone, onto projectile shafts. Other parts, those that I consider inedible, are discarded. Am I a criminal?

Cultures other than my own, gleefully retain stomach linings, uteri, and many other parts, that are generally considered waste products by most hunters. What parts to retain, and what to discard are personal decisions, and none of the state's business, yet many such decisions, are by definition, considered crimes.

Crow and coyote hunting is popular in some areas, as is shooting rock-chucks and other species considered by many to be non-edible. Almost always these animals are left intact in the field, or only their pelts are retained.

It is apparently unlawful to waste edible parts of some animals but not others: yet nowhere are exceptions to the wastage laws referenced in any regulations.

One hunter may be less skilled than another when it comes to processing their harvested meat, causing waste. Therefore, many are subject to wastage law violations, if this law were interpreted literally. This fact demands that enforcing such laws are done so subjectively, where it should be done objectively!

My point is, that once again WDFW dictates their own ethics, and ignores those of other cultures when making laws. (Racists perhaps?)

In my opinion, wastage laws are unenforceable in their current form. If a game animal is lawfully harvested and possessed, the hunter and his party should be able to use the entirety of the carcasses any way they see fit.

According to current law, if game meat is *"gifted"* to another, the gift must be accompanied by a *"possession statement"*. Yes, that includes a stick of homemade peperoni at Christmas! That's a little much isn't it?

Few of these regulations make any sense! Possession statements should be required while the wild game product is in the field, but when it's at home and or processed, no. This is a very easy fix that WDFW has not yet considered.

Parts that are useful and or edible to some are not so to others. How is it that WDFW can make this decision for you?

My thoughts regarding wastage are very unpopular with some hunters and wildlife professionals alike.

Yet, if one were to spend some time thinking about it, it is likely that they would come around to my way of thinking.

"A political culture of any given society is the major cause of conflict, hence, a key to its settlement as well." (Jochen Hippler)

26

The death of Bullwinkle

Not long ago a large bull elk assumed a very visible lifestyle near, and sometimes within, the central Washington town of Ellensburg. Year after year, he grew larger, to the point that he no doubt was the devil upon the shoulder of nearly every poacher in the area.

Named *"Bullwinkle,"* by the local media, he grew more and more confident in hobby farmer fields and nearby yards. He was protected by hunting regulations that appeared on their surface to make sense. More specifically, the area was technically open to hunting, but only for what the WDFW regulators considered to be *"true spike"* elk, and only very seasonally at that. Bullwinkle was safe, or so it seemed.

WDFW has a program in place where ordinary folks can enter a lottery (for a cash fee) and if extremely lucky may win a chance to kill *"Any Bull Elk"* during any open elk season, for a lawful elk. The minimum standards for the elk to be hunted is different depending upon the area hunted. It is called by some the *"Governors Tag."* Although the Governor publically denied knowledge of this when the shit hit the fan. (If a trophy elk tag was named after me, I would remember it.)

One very avid, and I might add wealthy, elk hunter. One known to push the envelope from time to time, and to spend a great deal of money to enhance elk hunting opportunities in general, purchased $70,000 worth of lottery chances. He won the much coveted Governors Tag, fair and square.

BOOM! Bullwinkle was killed, in view of many. Then he was hastily transported whole to an area open to hunting large bull elk. This act confirmed to the investigating officers that the shooter was aware of the illegality of his actions.

There was a public uproar. All hunters took the heat while anti-hunters celebrated and WDFW cashed the check. Diligent Fish and Wildlife Officers took the bull by the horns (forgive the pun), seized Bullwinkle's head and hide and put together what appeared to be a very good elk poaching case. We officers discussed it at length. It was a solid case we all agreed. However, some quietly wondered if the published regulations would hold up to the scrutiny of the courts. We all knew, and in fact had complained about some of the language regarding the definitions of a "*true spike*," and *"three point or better."* Despite the hard work of the officers involved, the apparent righteousness of their actions, near total public support and the intent of the law. And due to excellent defense lawyer work, with a little help from a questionable court ruling, the case was dismissed. The head and hide were returned to the hunter.

Had an experienced officer been consulted and listened to, when the definitions regarding antler points were made, I believe a conviction would have been obtained, or the shooter would have not recognized the weakness in the law in the first place.

Anti-hunters and non-hunters alike, perceived that this act was typical of hunters in general. Numerous WDFW Commissioners no doubt took advantage of this perception, and saw it as further motivation to phase out hunting. I absolutely believe this!

    RIP Bullwinkle

27

Wolves in Washington (A Myth?)

Once again let me bring up Captain Merriweather Lewis and Lt. William Clark. These men were tasked by the President of the United States to explore the interior of North America with an eye to establish the most convenient cross country trading rout possible. In addition, they were to document scientific discoveries regarding natural flora and fauna as well as indigenous peoples they encountered along the way. Many new and wonderful discoveries were made and all were well documented.

Many animals, new to science were discovered including pronghorn antelope, prairie dogs, big horn sheep and wolverine. Fish were collected and described, including Cutthroat Trout, Coho Salmon and Columbia River smelt. Their scientific discoveries were vast, and many species carry their names today. (Notably *Oncorhynchus clarkia,* AKA Cutthroat Trout.) Other species, already known to science were meticulously described as well, using scientific nomenclature, albeit in Lewis and Clarke's own form of spelling. (They have had a huge influence upon me.)

On the Great Plains, wolves were seen in great numbers and were similarly described to include several types. Also they wrote about the *"burrowing wolf".* Neither wolf, nor dog, although bearing a resemblance to both, they were clearly referring to what we all now know as coyotes. I found their descriptions of the "white bear" (Grizzly) particularly graphic.

While hauling thousands of pounds of gear and several boats across country, while trying to establish trade and relationships with Indian tribes, these men stayed very busy with many other things, including gathering food, general survival and scouting potential routes west. They never for a moment however, stopped making observations of the animals that they encountered.

Interestingly, when reading their journals, any reference of wolves, abruptly stopped at the Great Falls of the Missouri, only to resume when at the same point on their return journey.

Once the expedition entered what is now Washington State, elk became nonexistent, as did white-tailed deer. (Both species however reappeared when they arrived at Fort Clatsop. This is well documented.) Suddenly, however, cougars were documented. (Lewis and Clark didn't miss much.) Their observations of animal species were especially keen. The survival of the expedition depended upon it, and diligence in documenting their observations was ordered by the President of the United States!

Absent were any references to wolves when they were in what is now Washington State, but many animals like California condors, Sea otters, and several species of salmon were documented. They continued to see *"burrowing wolves."* Remarkably, their observational skills were so astute, Meriwether Lewis noted that *"Salmon Trout,"* his term for steelhead, had fewer than 12 rays in the anal fin, distinguishing it from a salmon!

Wolf sightings were specifically documented on 59 days of the expedition, none while in what is now Washington State or Oregon.

When I make this point to a **WDFW** wolf advocate, they point out that Quileute and Makah people, spoke of the presence of wolves in their lore and depictions on totem poles. They forget, or perhaps never knew, that Washington Indians did not have totem poles, but that was a commonality to the west coast of British Columbia, Canada. Indian lore spoke of a highly stealth and intelligent dog-like creature that lived among them. A coyote or a wolf, we will never know? Even so, it is doubtful that an aboriginal carver would have distinguished them from domestic dogs, (They had many), or a coyote. Translating the unwritten language of the Indians into English was extremely problematic. No doubt many subtle meanings were missed altogether. Wolf or coyote? Imagine the game of charades played over that one!

Makah and Quileute tribal lore refer to a *"wolf dance"* and carved masks allegedly depicting wolves. Be aware that these tribes were known to be historically related to western Canadian tribes that really did have wolves! (**AKA** Sea Wolf, a small version of Gray wolf, living on coastal islands. A distinct sub species, far different than those inhabiting Washington State now. They eat primarily marine proteins.)

When I point this out to a wolf advocate, he switches gears and says that early settlers documented wolves in western Washington, and very quickly, prior to about 1900, killed nearly all of them.

I will then say, that most of these folks were European immigrants, most likely with a poor grasp of the English language. They would have known about wolves all too well, and no doubt brought their prejudices regarding wolves with them. Yet they likely did not distinguish between wolves and coyotes because their native language would not have the proper words for a coyote. Any dog like creature killing their chickens or their newborn calf, hence became wolves.

By now the wolf advocate is getting pretty pissed at me and called me a fascist. I control my temper, because this is when one knows they are winning an argument with a progressive thinking scientist. (A true scientist must be neutral and flexible in their beliefs, lest they are bias.)

I ask the wolf person to show me any physical proof that wolves were in Washington. (I am setting a trap for him of course.) He bites, and says that Hudson Bay records clearly document wolf pelts being processed through Fort Okanogan. Their records were very well kept and inarguable, he says. That's when I spring the trap and explain that it is so, but that Fort Okanogan was moving furs south at the time and that these records no doubt were from Canadian Wolves. Their origin is unknown. I follow up with a question. *"I have looked at the trapping records at Fort Nisqually retained by the Hudson's Bay Company no wolves were documented".* Ditto Fort Vancouver. This is about where the discussion usually ends, with me being called a fascist once more.

All I need is one confirmable case where wolves lived in western Washington. Just one! I know there were mastodons, saber tooth cats, sloths, and even a rhinoceros found imbedded in a Grant County lava flow. Why is it so difficult to show me a plausible record of a wolf?

Let me digress a little. There is no doubt that wolves were re-introduced into Idaho some time ago and that their progeny are rapidly expanding in Washington. The DNA proves it! But, one must be aware that this particular stock of wolf originated someplace in the interior of Canada, and could not represent the type that were originally here, if, in fact, there ever were any.

Where the wolf lover scores points in this debate is that it has been documented that western Canadian wolves would have no trouble crossing the U.S.-Canadian border. But we also know now that the vast majority of Washington wolves are descendants from the Idaho re-introductions.

Don't get me wrong! I believe that there is a place in Washington for introduced wolves. Just like there is now a place for the many species of non-native fish and game birds, albeit known to be invasive.

Also, for the record, I can examine my own argument, find fault with it, and recognize that there were almost certainly wolves in what is now Washington State. This opinion seems to be supported by Clallam County wolf bounty records that I have recently seen. I find some of these records dubious for several reasons. First of all, they appear to be typed copies of hand written records, totally inadmissible in any courtroom without the originals. (I however, can provide hand written documentation of paid seal bounties from the 1960s.)

There seems to be a nine year gap between the last wolf allegedly inspected and the last bounty paid, and almost all of the bounties, were paid to only three households. No records that I can find, exist in Grays Harbor County, (once known as Chehalis County and included the county of Lewis,) or for any other western Washington county. Poor record keeping is a possible explanation. So is the possibility of a corrupt bounty system where cash was paid on misidentified coyotes or ended up in the local game protector's pocket.

More reliable reports from the descendants of pioneering families, strongly suggest wolves were here however. To what extent, we will never know.

Certainly however, assuming that wolves were here in Washington, they were related to the current form by a technicality only. We will never understand exactly what their role was or how they interacted with elk and deer of their day. What we know for certain is that there were historically far fewer elk and deer here, than at present.

Imagine WDFW's response if it were to be suggested that Green River Chinook salmon, were to be transplanted into the upper Columbia. The terms *"bad science, irresponsible, unlawful, idiotic,"* would come screaming out of the mouths of every WDFW Commissioner. *"We can't do that. It is totally against the ESA!"* Yet, central Canadian wolves, relocated to the Yellowstone area, rapidly expanding into Washington, is a success? My god, what are these people smoking?

The biological accident regarding wolves is considered a huge success story by many WDFW Commissioners. Wolf presence in the state of Washington now demands much attention, money and personnel, and they serve to distract the general public from many far more important conservation issues. It remains a mystery to me exactly how WDFW can claim a success from an accident when many other similar accidents are, in fact, documentable failures.

"I would thoroughly love to see a wolf in the wild here in my home state, or even to hear one howl. Just as I would love to feel the pull of, and see the excited flash of, a leaping Atlantic salmon on the end of my line." (Author quote)

(28)

Things that WDFW does well

In spite of it all, WDFW is highly skilled, and yields a superb work product with some endeavors. Yes, there are some things that they are <u>very</u> good at.

The hatchery program within WDFW, when used correctly, is a well-oiled machine and second to none in the world. The men and women so employed are experts in what they do and take pride in their work despite their relatively low pay. The citizens of the state of Washington, and WDFW management, need to recognize that potentially, their ultimate work product creates far more revenue, in the form of contributions to commercial and sport fisheries, tourism, tackle and boat sales, excise tax, etc., than what is spent by the tax payers. Bluntly said, hatchery business is good business. It's a *"cash cow"* that the state of Washington does not recognize.

With one arm tied behind their backs, and with revisions to current law (like ESA,) the men and women of the hatchery program alone could shut up guys like me forever. (I would be too busy fishing and Orca would be breeding like rabbits.)

Those that manage quality trout fishing opportunities in eastern Washington do a wonderful job as well, partially due to the fact that those folks are somewhat insulated from the many regulatory ambiguities that west side salmon and steelhead managers are so enamored with.

If one goes on-line, he or she can view numerous and beautifully produced fishing tutorials giving *"how to"* tips regarding fishing for locally abundant species like Lake whitefish, and burbot. The wonderful WDFW employees that produce these films are the very few that truly understand the value of promoting recreational opportunity in this state. We need far more like them.

Those efforts that focus upon introducing our youth to fishing and hunting could do a great job if properly funded. WDFW relies upon citizen volunteers for much of this work, and this fact should be better acknowledged, if not rewarded.

Perhaps the best success story is that of our very own razor clam managers. They consistently produce and maintain a wonderful fishery totally unique to the state of Washington that adds to the quality of life to all involved.

Even our Dungeness crab managers successfully manage what appears to be a renewable resource that pleases many thousands of both commercial and recreational fishers. They provide much needed revenue for both participants and local businesses. Marine areas 13 and 12, (South Puget Sound & Hood Canal,) being notable exceptions.

Put and take trout fisheries, maintained largely by our own hatchery program, pleases many thousands of less serious anglers. However, our collective, overall quality of life is improved, and much needed license revenue is created.

Most, if not all, other successful WDFW operations appear to this writer to be biological accidents.

"Sometimes, although fleetingly, I see hope." Author quote.

Disappearing ink

Well known to all Washington fishing and hunting license holders is the fact that licenses are printed with disappearing ink! A few months in a wallet, exposed to the sun, the heat of a car dash board or a drop or two of rain water, and the document bleaches out and assumes the appearance of cheap toilet paper. Many times, while enforcing WDFW Parking Permit compliance, I observed totally blank license documents, prominently displayed on cars. For most anglers, reading the print on their catch records cards is impossible a month into the season. The only legible writing on it, is their own notations on what was caught! Yes, legible notations in ink are required for this seemingly important legal requirement, but not so, it seems, for WDFW! The irony being that the ink on a citation works just fine!

Often, enforcement officers, do not write infractions for failing to record catch for this very reason. I once recall seeing a student officer insisting that an angler sign, in ink, his fishing license. Clearly this new guy had read the regulations and was trying to do a good job. Out of view of the angler, we *"had the talk."* Call it the facts of life if you will. *"Some laws are just total bullshit,"* I said.

WDFW administrators are so out of touch, they have no idea what a laughing stock they truly are.

"WDFW is a katagelasticists dream!" (Author Quote)

A true story regarding total WDFW incompetence

WDFW is very fond of holding regional meetings where employees get together and listen to agency leaders speak. Such meetings were always mandatory for enforcement officers but I never recall being asked to participate.

One particular meeting was led by the deputy director of the agency with the real director sitting nearby at another table. With a microphone in hand, the second in command at WDFW started with the basic, *"You're all doing a great job!"* speech. (This, despite the group's total awareness that things within the agency were not going well and one high ranking manager was going to prison.) He then launched into a doom and gloom fiscal situation, which often seemed to be the case. He spoke of having his hands tied by the low cost of licenses. He expressed his efforts to raise license fees and how he would spend the money. This guy knew so little about salmon and fish and game in general, he made perhaps the dumbest statement that I had ever heard! Remember, this was voiced by the supervisor of every salmon biologist in the room and there were many!

He said, very clearly, that fishing license sales are lagging, but that we should be able to more than make up for this deficiency with this coming summer's expected huge Pink salmon run!

Now in his defense, the prior summer, because of a biological *"accident,"* we had seen an unanticipated Pink salmon run, so far off the scale of normalcy that it caught the entire agency, and many thousands of happy anglers totally off guard! Some streams that historically got only a few dozen Pink salmon, saw millions! This, as yet unexplained, *"bio accident,"* of course had spiked the previous year's license sales.

Unknown to this *"expert,"* yes the deputy director of WDFW, was the fact that Pink salmon only return to Washington streams in odd numbered years. Everyone else in the room knew that this year's Pink salmon run would be zero. He had also mistakenly believed that the previous Pink salmon run was normal! This, despite the fact that he had already served through at least two prior Pink salmon runs with very low returns. Apparently, the second in command at WDFW knew nothing about salmon.

A silence spread across the room as if an altar boy cut a fart. This guy was already spending the money that would be generated by increased license sales that were not going to happen! The real director caught the error, grabbed the microphone, and as best as he could started walking back his cohort's statement much like the Whitehouse does when the President says almost anything.

I was very embarrassed for him, but at the same time, wondered why none of the many salmon managers present felt the need to say anything. Were they afraid to do so, or did they just not care? I realized at that moment, that we were all in deep trouble.

"Standards in public life have decayed over time...Incompetence is the norm." (Jed Mercurio)

An overview

Approximate 641,000 fishing licenses were sold in the state of Washington in 2020, and a lesser number of hunting licenses. By my calculations that's .085 fishing licenses per capita. (I have to be careful here because my accumulative college GPA is only 2.01) As you can see, anglers represent a small minority of the state's population. You can add to these numbers a little by being aware that juveniles don't need a fishing license at all. However, I suspect that many of these license holders buy shellfish / seaweed licenses only, realistically shrinking the true number of total anglers. (Seaweed licenses and managing algae? There's another chapter!)

The average angler dusts off and organizes grandpa's tackle box once or twice per year and drowns a few worms (illegally it seems) seeking put- and- take hatchery trout. If he catches a few crappie or other non-natives along the way, all the better. Many anglers passionately target bass in the very rich bass waters of eastern and western Washington, seeking nothing else. Because of shrinking opportunities involving salmon and steelhead, others become obsessed with walleye or the very abundant warm water non-native species readily available through a series of biological accidents that WDFW takes credit for.

Inland anglers, those that focus on the highly productive lakes in eastern Washington or the upper Columbia River, including Lake Chelan, Moses Lake, Banks Lake and the like, tend to not pursue saltwater salmon, ground fish and steelhead, where most of the complex fishing regulations exist. Fly fishing purists, those seeking solitude, quality catch and release fishing, and low angler density also remain relatively less impacted by bad regulations.

My point is, that even though anglers represent a small percentage of the overall population in Washington, the number of anglers negatively affected by conflicting, absurd, and ambiguous regulations is, generally speaking, limited to the remaining passionate, and obsessed if you will, salmon, steelhead and marine fish anglers on the west side of the state.

Those passionate anglers indoctrinated to fishing at the truly magical and historic fishing areas in western Washington are the most screwed, as are those that fish the lower Columbia, Westport, La Push, Neah Bay, Sekiu, Pillar Point, Port Townsend, Possession Point, Foul Weather Bluff, Point No Point, and on and on to south Puget Sound.

Anglers who crowd coastal rivers and streams, those in southwest Washington, and the entire Puget Sound Basin, where most Washingtonians live, assume the brunt of the conservation burden, and therefore are the most victimized.

Each regulatory issue, and there are hundreds, are managed by different entities and individuals. It appears to me that they do not communicate. I find this surprising because communication has never been easier due to advances in technology.

"It's as if a bunch of cooks are standing around a pot of boiling seawater, each dumping in ingredients without thought for what the other is dumping in. The guy in charge of the fire, has the right idea, but the one in control of the lid is working

from home, so the pot boils over, leaving most of the stew on the floor." (G. Haw to the current Wildlife Commission,)

Let's get a mop, get rid of the cooks, and instead hire a chef!

We west side anglers are far more victimized than the warm water fish or trout angler. I don't have the data, telling me how many of us there are. A few hundred thousand I would guess, based upon license sales. Unfortunately, we are not enough to influence any election, so why would the governor be concerned about us? (Sad, but true.) So we are forced to rely on the WDFW Commission to understand our position. In their current form, we are without hope.

It seems that the more fish are managed, the more complex the regulations must be, and I understand that. Therein exists a far higher public expectation that the regulators get it right, and WDFW management has failed in this endeavor, miserably.

Once again I feel compelled to remind the reader that the enforcement program, those who understand the repercussions of *"bad regulations,"* are not even invited to regulatory meetings. Managers will, from time to time request input. But in my 34 years of experience, it is *ignored.*

"I have not failed, I've just found 10,000 ways that won't work." (Thomas Edison)

Fishing is important, even for the occasional angler. Without an experienced mentor, or even with one, a citation is all too likely

(32)

Fishing with a professional guide or on a charter boat

Guides and charter boats provide a very valuable service. Novice anglers, and many skilled ones too, often choose to pay a professional to take them fishing. The guides local knowledge is vast as are their angling skills. When hiring a guide or charter boat, a high quality trip filled with many lifetime memories is almost guaranteed. Very often, when going with a professional, the customer does not know where he will be fishing. The guide has not decided yet. The customer relies on the experience of the guide, the availability of fish, river or weather conditions and of course his knowledge of the local regulations.

If we can't expect the enforcement officer to know the rules how can we expect the fishing professional to know? Given the current state of affairs, in our world of sudden emergency closures, and nonsensical written regulations, the guide or charter skipper is vulnerable to getting a ticket as are his or her paying customers. With that comes a high degree of embarrassment for all involved.

Most recreational fishing violations are what we call "*civil infractions.*" There is a very low burden of proof associated with them. They are unlike "*criminal citations*" where the burden of proof *is* extremely high, "*reasonable doubt.*" With infractions however, if the violator "*most likely*" committed the violation, he will probably be found guilty.

Let's say the guide, charter skipper, or even the bait boy, unknowingly rigs the customer up with an unlawful barbed hook, a prohibited bait, or violates a myriad of other potential infractions. The customer is liable for the ticket, not the person who is truly responsible. Yes, the visitor from Texas who bought a two day license that same morning, gets the ticket!

A real-life violator contact with a guide went like this:

The Olympic peninsula stream was suddenly burdened with a regulation prohibiting anglers from fishing from a boat. They were allowed to exit the boat and fish, but prohibited from fishing from the boat itself. This law clearly cramped the way boat fishing guides did their business. It essentially prohibited taking novice anglers fishing who were unable to effectively wade, perhaps old or impaired in some way or unable to cast the temperamental level wind reels.

An officer observed a guide boat, with two paying customers happily fishing from a boat. Their rods were in holders, lines were deployed. It was a clear violation of the law and the officer directed the *"suspects"* to row to shore and submit to a catch and gear inspection. What the officer saw were two folded up wheel chairs in the bow of the boat! Both men were disabled Iraq war veterans, true heroes, celebrating having survived the war!

Clearly, the officer did not issue a ticket. Instead he explained the new law and its intent. One hero said, *"Well, we clearly can't get in and out of the boat very easily. When we booked this trip, we had no idea that one couldn't fish from a boat. Can we fish the rest of the day, we traveled a long way to do this?"* The officer, stuck between a rock and a hard place, was forced to explain his interpretation of the law. Fishing from a boat was specifically prohibited. The Officer had to admit that the powers that be, made no concession for what was an obvious and easily anticipated issue. (A citation was NOT issued.)

Soon after, a rumor circulated around the town of Forks. The water Nazi had terminated the war heroes fishing trip! Not true, but that's the way it was interpreted by the locals.

I blame the idiot WDFW Commission members, and the *"woke"* steelhead biologists. Yes the same ones that have repeatedly refused input from the enforcement officers. Once again the Fish Cop takes the heat!

"Blaming the Fish Cop for bad regulations is like cutting off the tail of the rattlesnake. He can still bite, and now he's pissed off. " (Author quote)

<h1 align="center">(33)</h1>

Enforcement officer training

I spent a large part of the last twenty years training new officers both in the field and in a classroom setting. In that manner I was able to influence perhaps 70 officers, mostly still active. Many went on to outrank me, including a deputy chief, two captains and too many sergeants to count, and I am proud of that.

The current regulation pamphlet is largely useless for officer training, except to teach student officers caution, and to remind them that the rule makers and commissioners don't know what they are doing. (So I guess it has some value.)

 I recall with a laugh, once searching the enforcement office for a regulation pamphlet at the Chiefs' request. He was on an important phone call with an influential politician seeking answers regarding fishing regulations. I nervously reported back, that try as I might, I could not locate a fishing regulation pamphlet in the entire enforcement office. The Chief responded, *"Fuck it, they are worthless anyhow,"* and went back to his call.

 (I could not even find a regulation pamphlet in the enforcement office! That's an example of how worthless they really are!)

As you can tell, I have been a critic of the regulation pamphlet for many years. I took every opportunity to train new officers regarding the potential pitfalls. The best training tool that I used was taking the student officer hunting and or fishing. Yes, with a fishing rod or rifle in one hand and a regulation pamphlet in the other, student officers were required to wade through the regulatory muck and come out at the other end without violating the law.

Those without an outdoor background in Washington State, and there were many, found their field training experience eye opening and confusing. Some never got it and were terminated. I would tell them that their minimum knowledge base must exceed that of the average hunter / angler. I found this to be an unrealistic goal because most of one's resource knowledge is established very early in life, and without exposure to real issues, complete understanding is near impossible. Proper perspective takes time and experience. The twelve week, new officer field training program is appropriate for the police agencies that it was designed for, but it is unrealistic in a job that drastically changes seasonally. An elk season patrol, for example, cannot be replicated in the spring, nor can an ocean salmon patrol be conducted in the fall of the year.

The reality remains, that not only must the veteran officer's knowledge far exceed that of the most informed angler/hunter, it must similarly exceed that of prosecutors, judges and defense attorneys. Exceeding that of the folks who make the rules, is painfully easy.

"Wisdom often comes from a total lack of training, especially when proper training is impossible." (Author quote)

(34)

Deceptive practices if not outright lies

The recreational fishing pamphlet clearly advertises fishing opportunities that do not exist. Some species listed as *"open"* for fishing, realistically do not exist largely due to years and years of poor management.

Let me just touch on a few examples keeping in mind my vast experience with these issues. I have interviewed many others who are *"In the know"* including a select, albeit small, group of trusted biologists.

Regarding Marine Area 13 as published on Page 131 of the regulation pamphlet:

> ➤ **Year round season for Steelhead:**

I have never checked an angler with a steelhead, nor have I ever heard of one caught in Marine Area 13.

> ➤ **Year round Sturgeon:**

 I have never seen nor heard, of a sturgeon being caught in Marine Area 13. To advertise a year round season is deceptive.

- ➢ Mackerel:

Although I caught one once in south Puget Sound, it was an anomaly. Because of a bio accident, they were thick as fleas one summer at Sekiu, but I have never heard of another angler ever catching a mackerel in Marine Area 13! To advertise a year round season, with no bag limit is deceptive.

- ➢ **Pacific cod, Pollack, hake and wolf eel are listed as "open year round" (Catch and release)**

I saw Pacific cod back in the 1970s and pollack were abundant back then. I am aware of a single documented take of a wolf eel. I have not seen any of these species in Marine Area 13 during my entire time as an enforcement officer. (34 years) Again, this advertised fishing opportunity is misleading.

Until recently, there was an advertised halibut season in this area, although none have ever been recorded to my knowledge. Also albacore were once advertised as open with no bag limit! These intentional promotions were outright lies. And it's not like I'm not looking! I have documented many rare and obscure fish in marine area 13, including Pacific Rag fish, Pacific Lancet fish, Catalina croaker, Seven gill cat sharks, Pacific barracuda, Blue shark, Basking shark, Salmon shark, Ocean sunfish, a handful of Plainfin midshipmen, and a Sturgeon sea poacher, but NEVER a steelhead, halibut, sturgeon, or albacore!

I can only assume that these exceedingly rare species outnumber many of those that are advertised as open year round!

I can go on and on and make similar commentary with all the marine areas and sub areas. I will spare the reader the redundancy. I use area 13 as an example because it is the area that I have the most experience with.

In fact, just today 03/21/2022, WDFW announced a halibut season in Marine Areas 9 and 10. Not a single halibut will be landed in area 10, although I'm sure a few flounders will be misidentified and perhaps a skate or two. Very few, perhaps none, will be landed in Area 9. What's more, WDFW knows it! Catching a coelacanth is just as likely as catching a halibut in Marine Areas 10, 11, 12 and 13.

 I don't know what the author of these *"opportunities"* got for writing them, but he should have gotten 10 years in the pen! He could have falsely promoted more fishing opportunity there.

"Liar, liar, pants on fire." (Author quote)

*"Justice will take over fabricators of lies and false witnesses."
(Heraclites)*

Fish handling rules

As mentioned earlier many species of fish and often unclipped salmon and steelhead must be released. The result being arbitrary fish handling restrictions, but for some reason, depending on the area where one is fishing, restrictions depend on how big your boat is. Once again the smaller boats, the anglers that have less money, generally speaking, have more restrictions than the rich. Does the Commission have any idea?

They even have imposed fish landing rules on species that can by law be retained. (In some areas one cannot use a gaff hook to land even a lawful fish intended to be retained.)

> ➢ **MARINE AREA 5 through 13: Unlawful to bring a wild salmon or a species of salmon aboard a vessel if it is unlawful to retain that salmon.**

Coho, pink or sockeye may be kept at any size. It's pretty hard to determine if a small fish is clipped or not, let alone what species they are, without close inspection and bringing them into a boat. It's clear to me that those who make the rules don't go fishing! (Only chinook have a minimum size.)

Fish handling rules also differ depending on areas fished within the lower Columbia River, again with a large boat exception. (Page 12)

Once while patrolling a tribal halibut fishery in Marine Area 6, I observed a commercial long liner pulling his gear. I saw many undersized halibut gaffed, yes impaled on a large hook, and then released. I was shocked, yet I was advised by the local officers that this was a normal practice in this fishery.

So far, I have resisted the temptation to cross over into the commercial or tribal regulations. Wild fish caught in gill net fisheries disturb me as well. These issues are for another writer and another book.

The best way to get a bad law repealed is to enforce it strictly.

(Abraham Lincoln)

A small boat angler, desperately trying to unwrap a wild fish without hurting it. Yes, netting it was required. A violation of state law!

(36)

Recreational fishing regulations favor the wealthy

For many thousands of recreational anglers in Washington State, procuring low cost, high quality food is as much of a motivation to go fishing as anything else.

Most certainly, for almost all anglers, getting something to eat is a good thing, but not for all. Bass anglers are not motivated by eating their catch. In fact in many bass tournaments, if a fish dies, the angler is penalized. Ditto for the fly fishing purist. He or she has a highly refined fishing ethic where harming the fish, other than hooking it, is unthinkable. Even a photograph of his catch is done so with the greatest of care. Yet for the masses, eating fish for dinner, or smoked salmon at Christmas is a major part of their constitutionally guaranteed right to the pursuit of happiness.

I crunched a few numbers, and without getting into any real detail I can say that I spend about ten percent of all money earned on fishing/hunting related pursuits... at least. If I saved that amount, over the course of my career, over and above pension contributions, I would be a wealthy man now. I didn't, and I'm not, because I like to fish and hunt too much.

Clearly, many wealthy folks like to fish and hunt too. The ten percent of their income that they spend, is far greater than mine. Should they be more entitled to a very limited recourse than I?

Boat and vehicle gas alone cripples me. Add to that the cost of non-ethanol fuel required for modern outboards, even small ones, and to the outlandish cost of *"marina gas,"* not to mention the current $5.80 / gallon price, I have to plan each trip carefully. Salmon openings are often very limited windows of opportunity, that open and close on the whim of fish managers. Bad weather is something I can live with, but I am far more likely to take that risk if I knew the season was closing in a few days. Often, small boat anglers like me are compelled to go fishing when it is not safe to do so.

Lodging, food, bait, licenses, permits, travel time, gear, the list is endless. My annual retirement income is simply not enough to pursue my passion, even moderately. Imagine the restrictions so placed on hard working folks that make far less than I!

Pursuing halibut and salmon 20 miles offshore remains a pipe dream. Towing a small boat to the mouth of the Columbia River, for a day or two of fishing is cost prohibitive.

Yes, I believe that the way fish are managed, wealthy people, who tend to be white I might add, take the far greater, and disproportionally large share of the available resource. The fishing and hunting regulations assure this! As mentioned earlier, in many areas, expensive electronics and far more expensive gear is required to stay oriented in open areas, further prohibiting fishing by the less wealthy.

Yet the poor man's license fees are identical to the rich mans.

Fishing was once not like that. I believe that being able to go fishing or hunting for low cost, quality food, is the value that interested hunters and anglers in the first place. It should be at least considered by the bean counters in charge.

An angler or hunter should be charged based on what he or she takes from the resource, not upon what he or she dreams about taking!

The opportunity to hunt or fish belongs to all, not just a privileged few.

Fish and wildlife managers, and the uninformed individuals that direct them, have it all wrong! Yet according to the current governor of the great state of Washington, poor folks and those with low credit ratings get all kinds of financial compensation. Unlawfully parking motor homes, pitching tents, cooking fires, and erecting semi-permanent structures on public property, encouraging criminal behavior, free crack pipes, and many other benefits are granted to the homeless. Hard working low income folks often struggle through life, yet the government goes to great lengths to improve their quality of life. Yet low income hunters and anglers, regardless of race, folks that are willing to work for low cost, high quality food, and a little recreation, are denied the opportunity at a rate far exceeding that of the wealthy. It's no wonder so many people feel compelled to cheat. And I can't blame them!

Would it be appropriate to call the WDFW Commission racist? Is the term *"white privilege"* applicable? *"Oh no, not us, that's absurd"* they scream! I believe that they are the most bias rule making body on earth well, in my world anyway.

Hopefully, this gets them thinking for a change.

"Anyone who has struggled with poverty knows how extremely expensive it is to be poor." (James Baldwin)

Low cost, high quality small boat experiences, have become rare. (Off shore Mid 1970s)

Small boat salmon fishing for the budget angler is becoming a thing of the past.

(37)

Equitable Estoppel

Before reading this section, I ask the reader to review my disclaimer at the beginning of the book. Once again I am not a lawyer and hold no qualifications to interpret law other than that of a lay person. If the reader needs clarification regarding this legal concept he or she should consult with a lawyer so trained, or with the Washington State Attorney General's Office. Even so, the ultimate decision regarding any interpretation remains with the presiding judge.

My interpretation of Equitable Estoppel is this:

If ambiguity exists in written form, in any law, or declaration where people are expected to lawfully comply, or in any written contract requiring abidance to expectations contained within it, the courts shall rule, (not may rule, but shall rule), in favor of the party that did not create the ambiguity. Even if it is found that the accused party committed the acts!

Ambiguity is defined as: When a single word or phrase may be interpreted in two or more ways.

This argument was made when courts were adjudicating Indian treaties and associated fishing rights. Because the treaty was written in a language containing only about 600 words, complex points contained within the treaty could not adequately be made, and of course Indians could not even read the text at the time of the signing. The courts, much later, had no choice but to rule in the treaty tribe's favor. (The ambiguity contained within the treaty was both patent and latent in nature. Much like the current regulations.)

Now, how does this affect the recreational angler who is expected to comply with ambiguous regulations, under penalty of incarceration, fines, and / or forfeiture of equipment?

Fishing related **RCW**s and **WAC**s remain somewhat clear to the trained legal mind, yet even **WDFW** sees the absurdity of anglers being forced to carry that monstrous stack of paperwork with them while fishing. (It's just not safe.) Yet I find the condensed version, **AKA**, the current recreational fishing regulation pamphlet, to be ambiguous almost in its entirety.

"The enemy of accountability is ambiguity."(Patrick Lencioni)

The regulation kiosk at Cabela's. I could kiss the guy who placed my *"bad regulation"* article there.

An unpopular idea

Long before I was an enforcement officer I was indoctrinated upon the idea that salmon snagging should be unlawful. My first enforcement efforts were to combat what I believed to be a very wasteful, indiscriminate, and un-gentlemanly way to fish. In those days, the vast majority of salmon fishing occurred in salt water areas where intentional snagging could not compete with lawful fishing. Not so in rivers, where schooling, non-feeding fish, were very vulnerable to this tactic.

Over time, as selective saltwater fishing became the norm, more and more marine salmon fishing opportunities became restricted or were entirely eliminated. The result being, huge surplus hatchery returns to some rivers. With that came an incentive for fish managers to remove these fish so that hatchery stocks would not mix with wild spawning stocks.

Harvestable fish, crowded in unnaturally small streams, still in prime condition but no longer feeding and difficult to catch, created quite the temptation for frustrated anglers.

The Puyallup river, Nisqually, Skokomish, Quilcene, Lewis rivers (and many more), began generating an unprecedented number of *"snagging complaints"* at a level unheard of before. The way WDFW dealt with this issue was to create *"anti-snagging"* rules, which are a collection of confusing regulations, involving hook sizes, types, lure buoyancy, weight positioning, presentation, and other things.

Each and every *"anti-snagging"* rule created a defense to the charge of snagging which was already against the law and easily proven. There was nothing wrong with original law.

 Again, biologists with no law enforcement awareness got involved and contradicted the anti-snagging intent, by allowing the retention of salmon if impaled *"On or near the head."* This essentially legalized the act of snagging which, ironically, served to greatly restrict the enforcement officer's ability to enforce any snagging regulations.

(Every experienced Fish Cop that I know predicted this at the time. We were ignored by management. The next time an angler complains about out of control snag fisheries, he or she should blame the out to lunch biologists, not the fish cops!)

Nobody hates a salmon snagger more than another salmon snagger. The vast majority of those that complain about it are the very same people that have perfected the act of what is now referred to as *"flossing." (Defined as snagging, while trying to appear legal!)*

However, concentrated, legal snagging could be a way of harvesting otherwise un-harvestable fish. As long as such areas were clearly defined and the act itself provided some degree of selection, there are places where such fisheries could, and should be allowed.

Currently there are tribal snag fisheries that run concurrently with non-tribal sport fisheries. Yes they are ugly, and few self-respecting true anglers would be caught dead there, but many would participate, and otherwise surplus fish could be utilized.

Yes, I am a proponent of establishing some designated snag fisheries. It has been done in Washington State in the past and it is a lawful mode of fishing in some great lake salmon streams. It is also tolerated in some Alaska sport and subsistence fisheries. It is wrong for one angler to place his or her fishing ethic upon another. However, hypothetically, if such a measure were ever adopted in Washington State, and an angler doesn't like it, he or she can choose not to participate.

Without spending too much more time on this topic, I would suggest calling lawful snagging opportunities *"subsistence fisheries."* Two perfect areas come to mind including the mouth of Minter Creek in marine are 13 and the Quilceen River below the hatchery weir. Some degree of snagging is already tolerated and tribal snagging is already allowed in both locations. Huge hatchery surpluses are a predictable annual event, and the fish are notably poor biters. Many other locations are great candidates for lawful snagging (subsistence) fisheries.

"What if WDFW decided to sell snag permits for such areas? I think they would sell like hot cakes!" (Author quote)

(39)

Confessional

I have discussed these issues with anyone that will listen, violators and non-violators alike. There have been thousands of anglers that been cited for a violation of the fish and wildlife code that had no idea that they were wrong...until it's too late. Such victims include people from all walks of life and include WDFW employees, and a surprisingly high number of high ranking ones at that.

I once landed a steelhead on *"bait"* in a stream with a bait prohibition. I released the fish, but I was unaware that I was a *"poacher"* until I got home. Yes, I was a fish cop at the time, and on my own beat. I had no idea!

I once went fishing on a rare day off out of Neah Bay. While letting out my line, in the dark of an early morning, I congratulated myself for beating the crowd. The instant a salmon grabbed my bait I realized that there was no one else fishing. Long story short, the season had closed at midnight, and I, the local fish cop had not gotten the word. This was very nearly a career ending mistake. If contacted, unlike anyone else, I probably would not have been cited, but I would have been in deep trouble. I dodged a bullet but remained very upset.

This last summer, with my 14 ft. boat I fished at Sekiu. I deployed my gear. The fishing was hot, but clipped, hatchery silvers were hard to find because of the high number of unclipped fish. In the blur of catching and releasing about 40 fish, my pal and I managed to retain two keepers. Aided by fog, a westerly drift, and a poor cell signal, I found myself 10 miles to the west of my starting point which was well into the closed area. (Have I cited folks for similar indiscretions? Yes I have, and now I must live with it.)

Being a former officer would not have protected me from a citation, particularly because by that time, I had become a rather outspoken opponent of *"bad regulations"* and had published numerous articles about it. Yes, I would have been a nice mount on someone's wall, along with many other familiar faces of current and former employees. (Including some that I have bad mouthed earlier in this document!)

Seeing as how I am an avid angler, and that regulations are getting far more complex each year, the likelihood that I and others like me will make similar mistakes is growing. It's a near certainty. We conscientious anglers, in my opinion, are more likely to get cited, caught so to speak, than the far less numerous outright bandits that ignore all regulation! (Bandits hide their actions. An angler unaware that he is violating, does not. And is therefore far more vulnerable)

If anyone should know these things, it's the very folks who make the regulations, and have made similar errors. Yet they remain nescient, because most are not passionate anglers/hunters. They tend to be bean counting, non-consumptive advocating, cop hating, climate change blaming, anti-hunting, bad regulation denying nincompoops. Which in my opinion, represents the entire makeup of non-enforcement higher ups and WDFW commission members.

The bottom line is that the agency, the Washington Department of Fish and Wildlife, just doesn't give a damn. WDFW, in published press releases, has stated unequivocally and repeatedly that the existing regulations are ambiguous and at times unenforceable. Their only attempt to fix this problem was the creation of a regulation app for smart phones. The problem with this effort is that the regulations sometimes are different depending on what kind of phone one has! And, that this system uses the same language as the regulation pamphlet itself!

Therein lies yet another slam dunk defense strategy for any real violator. Don't blame the courts for their dismissal of fish and wildlife cases....blame WDFW for making bad law!

"You know...confessing to avoid prosecution is a time-honored strategy." (Howard Taylor)

Sea weed license required and unlawful possession of unclassified marine invertebrates.

"Classifying anything as Unclassified, is the oxymoronic idea of a bad comedian, or worse, biologist." (Author quote)

Yes, a license from the WDFW is required to recreationally harvest seaweed. It appears that algae is managed right along with fish and big game. With every layer of new regulations comes more and more limitations and expense. Imagine the think tank that sits around dreaming up new ways to tax the citizenry, with the least amount of work. What is it exactly that the WDFW does to manage seaweed? Do they somehow control photo periods which would prompt more growth or enhance it in any way? There is a daily bag limit with a weight restriction. How did they determine a weight limit? Did they just pull a number out of thin air? Dry, damp or wet? Wrung out perhaps? I know of no place else on earth where algae has a bag limit and a license is required to collect it. Did the algae biologists somehow assess how fast it grows against how fast it's harvested? Why not possession limits? Let's add size limits while we're at it! I am not aware of any enhancement efforts or management strategies, regarding seaweed.

These laws are largely ignored by enforcement officers and are widely considered a bad joke among us. Nonetheless, many people, almost all of Asian descent and non-English speaking first generation immigrants, buy a license solely to harvest seaweed. These are the folks that are the least likely to complain, and the most likely to pay. I believe this is a law that disproportionately affects minorities. Back when the WDFW decided to regulate seaweed, I became certain that it was the beginning of the end. I was right!

Then the deluded dreamers at WDFW decided to prohibit possession of unclassified marine invertebrates. First they had to invent the concept with legislation. This catch-all classification is now defined by statute and includes far too many species to list here. Most associated species are so obscure that only a few highly educated marine biologists are even aware of them. The general public is aware of only a few. Let me put it this way, any beach walker returning to his or her car after a low tide beach walk, would have dozens of protected species clinging to their socks!

It is now a crime for a beach walker to pick up a sand dollar, a sea snail, a shore crab or any of the fascinating organisms encountered on a walk on the beach. An old, empty oyster shell in possession is unlawful, if removed from a public beach. Pile worms, sand fleas, and a myriad of other species are off limits even to the fascinated kid with dreams of becoming a marine biologist. (Perhaps current biologists don't want any competition and this is just an attempt at job security. There are many less plausible conspiracy theories out there.) It is a crime to pick up a sand dollar for crying out loud!

Let me put this is in the perspective that it deserves. The term *"bi-catch,"* applies to the unintentional take of marine organisms in fisheries across the globe. It is a major problem. A commercial bottom dragger for example, will harvest let's say, a ton of desirable species. After sorting three times that weight of undesirable or non-targeted fish will be discarded at sea. Yes, they are dead. Apply similar numbers to large catcher possessor fishing vessels on a global scale and one may be able to comprehend the scope of the problem. WDFW does not wish to address this issue, and largely ignores it. Instead, they elect to impress this concept upon the shore bound angler fishing from a dock or a family taking a walk at low tide! Again, the entire conservation burden is placed upon the recreational angler, (the kid on the dock) and the park visitor. Does WDFW really believe that the beach walker or dock fishermen has a larger impact on marine organisms than the commercial trawler who has no such restrictions?

The total lack of vision demonstrated by WDFW with nearly every conservation issue that I look at, over and over again, reflects a level of culpability that many would call criminal. Even the most forgiving observer would call it willful ignorance, extremely bad science or just simple bias. The phrase *"best available science,"* so in vogue with liberal minded politicians, in actuality often means just the opposite. How would WDFW's best available science apply, (minimizing hatchery stocks and their impact on wild) to wild Atlantic salmon recovery on the east coast of the United States? Well, it's been applied! They are functionally extinct.

Most developing urban anglers in my day learned how to collect potential bait after being fascinated by the sea perch and other fish, highly visible under any Puget Sound city dock. He or she soon learned that scraping barnacles off a piling created a feeding frenzy. Soon a hand line or cheap fishing rod were produced. Bits of debris from the piling was attached to a hook which was immediately stolen by an excited fish. The even more excited prospective angler/marine biologist, found a small critter that would stay on his hook. The inside of a mussel sufficed. A beautiful blue striped sea perch took the bait. The fish escaped but an angler was born. Soon other organisms more suitable for bait were discovered. Each seemed to work better than the previous one. My bait preference evolution started with a piece of barnacle, then a mussel. Tube worms, difficult to detach from under the dock, worked too. Shore crabs, far more easily collected and stayed on the hook, did not work as well. Finally, after much experimentation, pile worms, (Polychaeta) were discovered. The infant angler soon learned that they could inflict a painful bite, but was delighted to learn that they seemed to catch every fish that swam!

All but one of these species are now unlawful to possess. Mussels must be kept in a separate container and kept in the field in a condition so that they can be weighed. Breaking them apart to put on a fish hook is a crime.

"UN&%#&@#%BELIEVABLE!" (Author quote)

The best biologists/scientists in the world were made, making similar discoveries, as well as the best fish cops. Those days are gone. When WDFW says they are dedicated to promoting fishing opportunity, I cry like a child.

Prohibiting the possession of unclassified marine invertebrates was a regulation invented by a non-angler for sure, and a nonrealistic one at that.

I must also point out that there are many species that should be protected from unrestricted harvest that are currently *"classified as unclassified,"* although I hate using this oxymoronic language. WDFW needs to re-examine this issue in a way that makes sense, encourages some degree of recreational opportunity, yet remain reasonable. And yes, consulting with an experienced officer would be prudent.

What about a regulation that reads: *"A reasonable amount of live unclassified invertebrates may be collected and used for hook and line fishing bait. Please release excess specimens alive."*

Similar exceptions should be made for grasshoppers, crickets and of course angle worms.

"Apparently placing honest folks in a position to get arrested is far less important than preventing the accidental take of a few copepods." (Author quote)

(41)

The myth about Orca

Puget Sound resident Orca, by all accounts, number about 80 individuals. Associated news accounts always seem to emphasize suspected deaths over births, to the point that is a wonder that there are any left.

Some biologists have perpetrated the myth that our resident Orca eat primarily chinook salmon, over any other food source, and that their very survival is directly linked to chinook abundance.

WDFW, funded by federal dollars, spend millions enforcing marine mammal anti-harassment laws. They conduct many directed patrols for this purpose, even when the whales are known to be out of state which is a majority of the time. When present, WDFW Biologists send a great deal of time, chasing the whales around in small boats, waiting for one to defecate. If they are lucky, a fecal sample is collected with a dip net. The material is analyzed and BINGO, its chinook salmon tissue! It was quickly assumed by WDFW that chinook are the Orca's primary food source. Of course this news was embraced by Governor Climate Change, the tribes saw it as yet another way to restrict already highly curtailed non tribal fishing and WDFW saw it as a cash cow in the form of more federal grants. Let me point out a few problems with this kind of thinking.

All salmon experts agree, and there is no doubt, that chinook, are and have always been the <u>least</u> abundant species of pacific salmon, both in terms of numbers and relative biomass. Orca thrive in other regions of the world where salmon do not exist.

It does not make sense to me that an apex predator would evolve to specifically take advantage of a food source massively outnumbered by many other food sources that are far more available. While it is true that chinook salmon have a higher fat content than other species of pacific salmon, fat content varies within the species wildly, Spring Chinook having the highest levels, Tule chinook much lower for example. Other marine animals have far more, like herring and marine mammals.

Let's take a quick look at how WDFW Biologists determined that Puget Sound resident Orca are totally dependent on chinook for survival. As mentioned earlier WDFW Biologists chase around the friendly Orca's with especially designed "Pooper Scoopers" They wait for one to defecate, the material looking much like that of a sea gull. It is a liquid that ends up in a liquid, forming a faint whitish cloud. The biologist makes a frantic scoop with his fine meshed net and has his sample. The lab takes a look and Eureka! Its chinook salmon material.

This experiment is repeated and chinook salmon material shows up again and again. "It must be all that they eat!"

Governor Climate Change loves it! The tribes, who own him, love it, wildlife commissioners are ecstatic, the bio's get a big Atta Boy, a new federal grant and Bingo! , they have yet another great reason to further restrict non tribal recreational and commercial fishing. (They also have a great incentive to increase chinook hatchery production, but that reason is quickly quashed. The infinitely more expensive, and the least likely to work option, Snake River dam removal, gets to the top of the list!)

Now, remember that Chinook salmon have a much higher fat content than other pacific salmon. Fats and lipids are very buoyant, therefor after defecation, the original sample containing chinook salmon material would be much more buoyant that that of any other species of salmon in their diet. It is certain that material consisting of other species is less buoyant, and therefore probably sinks beyond the length of the pooper scooper. Unless the bio knows the total volume of the entire defecation, and the exact rate with which the material if processed internally, and the amount of fats withheld by the whale, making such a determination is highly suspect. Ask yourself: Is it possible that another determination could have been made if the bio had a longer net, or was a little slower on the scoop?

Another thing to consider is that our orca spend much, if not most of their time in areas far away. Often when our local chinook are the most abundant. What are they eating then?

In order for a theory to be determined as fact an experiment must be repeated and the results must be predictable. More than anything else data and materials collected must be done so as randomly as possible. WDFW takes advantage by biasing the science to get the results that they want. This perverts the results and makes for bad science. Paradoxically, it also helps them to obtain more federal grants for follow up studies, which is the real motivation for many modern scientific efforts. That's a problem!

The WDFW Biologists, whom I call "Turd Burglars," sometimes employ an intellect somewhat shorter than their scat nets.

"After 39 years working for this outfit, I have developed the habit of critical thinking.'" (Author quote)

(42)

Incompetence and the best available science

One again, in late August 2022, there occurred an event that is still in the process of playing itself out as of this writing. The Puget Sound salmon manager, Mark Baltzell decided upon an emergency salmon fishing closure in Marine Area 13, effective August 31[st,] 2022. Be aware that Marine Area 13 is advertised in the 2022 recreational fishing regulation pamphlet as being "Open Year Round for Salmon," the only marine area so listed. Now, it is well known that WDFW has the power to enact emergency closures when and if a conservation emergency occurs, which is all too commonly fabricated for political reasons. WDFW needs only to apply their "Best Available Science," (a standard often stated in formal press releases and commission meetings) then articulate and document an emergency justification. Then the Director has the enviable power to impose new law, without any legislation or oversight. It appears to this writer that a great deal of responsibility **should** be applied to this power.

Mark Baltzell works closely with Kyle Addicks, WDFW Intergovernmental Salmon Manager.

The justification given for this Marine Area 13 closure was low abundance of chinook, which even the uninformed knew to be false. Several area 13 terminal areas associated with two major chinook hatcheries were just starting to see great fishing as is historically the case. (Minter Creek and Deschutes Hatchery) Abundance in all other Marine areas had been sky high leading up to this. The long awaited arrival of Chinook by those who had to suffer through the great opportunities experienced by anglers up north, had finally happened. And yes, the highlight of my entire year, and that of many others was finally upon us!

Then BOOM! Marine Area 13 is closed by emergency order! Low abundance was the official justification, sparked by the tribal concern of late arrivals to the Nisqually River.

It's still August! Everyone knows that the chinook don't really enter the Nisqually River until the first rains of September. They hold up at Nisqually Reach and other nearby areas where anglers have an all too brief chance to catch them. This closure cannot be so! It's gotta be a typo!

I believe that tribal fishers, good folks that I have dealt with for 34 years, were concerned that the river was crowded with sport fishers getting in the way of tribal fishers. Few fish had entered the river as of yet, creating a stir amongst them which prompted a call to tribal leaders. They in turn, understandably, called WDFW citing concerns with tribal hatchery escapement goals.

Unbelievably, WDFW Salmon Manager, Mark Baltzell, decided to close all of Marine Area 13, including terminal areas at Minter Creek and Deschutes Falls hatcheries, for all salmon fishing! Unfathomably, leaving the Nisqually River wide open for sport fishing! (Be aware that in other areas where chinook fishing is closed, hatchery coho fishing remains open.)

This was a truly jaw dropping moment. Unbelievable to all. I called numerous retired fish managers and others that were aware of all the issues. They thought I was joking! "Your full of crap Greg, no one is that stupid!" Fish and wildlife enforcement officers were appalled.

Someone with more energy than I needs to file a "Public Disclosure Request" for any and all text message, phone calls and E mails, associated with this snafu; If you do you will either get a story bigger than Watergate, or rich as a result! Lets see them blame this boner on the pandemic or climate change!

Salmon manager Mark Baltzell, to his credit, incompetent yes, but clearly a man of integrity and under great pressure, fell upon his sword and took responsibility for the error. (Do not forget that Director Susewind signed off.)

Under greater pressure no doubt, managers at WDFW took lightning quick action, and lifted the closure. But not until hard earned vacation leave, prepaid moorage fees, and long awaited opportunity for already frustrated anglers was lost forever.

Apparently, Mark Baltzell's friends had reported to him that they had not been seeing fish on their fish finders, at least in part prompting the closure! (Is this their best available science?)

The reader must ask him or herself the following additional questions:

Q) Who signed off on this action?

A) The Director Kelly Susewind.

Q) What ever happened to the Best Available Science standard?

A) It does not exist, never did. It's a phony bullet point only.

Q) Who recognized the obvious error?

A) Not the commission, Director or his trusted advisors, but recreational anglers who are far better informed than salmon managers.

Q) If the Director signs off so easily on errors this obvious, what other erroneous and unjustified closures have been implemented?

A) Who knows?

Q) If gross misdemeanor crimes, such as fishing closed waters, result in arrest, who is liable to civil action and false arrest when the case is dismissed?

A) Not the folks that write them. But the Fish Cops that enforce them. (It should be the other way around.)

We anglers, as stewards of Washington State's natural resources, have a civic duty to point these and other obvious errors out. If not, shame on us!

"Never ascribe to malice that which is adequately explained by incompetence" (Washington Salmon Angler at any Washington State boat ramp.)

"Nothing, historically, distorts, perverts and therefore destroys science more than politics, religion and incompetence. In the case of WDFW, at least two out of three are in play." (Author quote)

(43)

Revenge

This fantasy, perhaps my favorite of many, goes something like this.

All the WDFW managers, director and commission members have read my latest book. They call a closed door meeting to discuss it. The commission chair is upset, "We have trouble" she says. She points her finger at the director and says, "How could you let this happen. This is embarrassing?

The director turns to the regional directors and shouts, "I trusted you guys with fixing this years ago. It appears you've done nothing."

The regional directors say, "We assigned this task to the managers. They have been working on it for years but because of climate change and covid-19, they forgot to do it."

The managers say, "Damn you guys. We know all about it. We have been telling you this might happen for years."

Things get out of hand. A regional director throws a low calorie doughnut at a manager.

The manager retaliates with a handful of granola, which covers many of the commissioners. Another launches a smoked oyster with an improvised covid mask slingshot directly into the face of the wolf biologist. Catered lunches come out and soon a chunk of tofu splatters across the glasses of a rather bookish looking fellow "I'm just here to take notes." he screams.

Several biologists take cover and arm themselves with staple guns. One accidently fires a staple into his thigh.

The director, heroically trying to regain control, screams, "I'm hit." He takes cover behind the power point projector. Pandemonium breaks out. Someone hits the fire alarm and others dive under the table.

The region six director is thinking, "I hope I deleted all of the e-mails that Officer Haw sent me, especially the ones where I said I agreed with him." He was last seen asking directions to the nearest shredding machine.

The fish program manager shouts, "Where is that son of a bitch enforcement chief? It's all his fault and that of his water Nazi thugs."

A cheer goes up in the room, then it falls silent...the Enforcement Chief wasn't invited to the meeting.

My fantasy will remain a fond day dream I'm sure. It is unrealistic to believe that improvements will be made based upon what I wrote because I have put it in writing so many times before. I even hand-delivered these ideas to the commission in the form of "free books" that cost me at the time about $10 each. The commission chair at the time responded verbally although not in writing. He agreed with everything I said but nothing was done.

Some, but not all of my prior chain of command, agree with me. Others consider my point's minutia, to be hashed out by attorneys at some future trial. What is sure to happen is civil litigation where the enforcing officer will be sued for applying these laws. Unfortunately, those responsible, will not be.

Hunters and especially anglers, will continue to be even more highly regulated. Hunting and fishing opportunity will continue to shrink. Many people will assume new pursuits as dictated by those in control.

I predict, if I meet my life expectancy without any major diversions, that I will become a bass enthusiast and give up on salmon and steelhead completely.

Thank god for biological accidents and the amateur *"bucket biologists,"* that provided them.

My hunting efforts, as long as the law allows, will be on my own property, guarded by a NO HUNTING sign. I will do so safely and avoid conflict with the anti-hunters that live across the road, but it won't be the same.

"If a law making body fears or denies the truth, there can be no justice." (Author quote)

Back yard buck! A glimpse at the future of hunting in
Washington State.

(44)

Last fantasy

There I am, minding my own business and having a great day of fishing. I get cited for an inadvertent fishing violation, no intent on my part, but I did it nonetheless. There's no doubt about it! It ruins my entire week. I am deeply embarrassed knowing that every current Fish and Wildlife Officer in the state will hear about it within minutes. The news will travel up the chain of command and back. The story will be embellished. (This has happened to another retiree that I know.) Some WDFW managers will high five one another. Even some of my prior civilian victims will rejoice. My picture will end up on a dart board in the commissioner's office. Worst of all my integrity will be breached, which is perhaps the worst part.

While despondent, I decide to pay the small fine and go about my life. I have an epiphany, No! I am going to apply all of my knowledge and beat this charge. I will do it for all the others who have failed to try. I'm going make my point if it's the last thing I do!

I appear at my arraignment and enter a plea of not guilty. I argue for a trial date as soon as possible. Then the hard part, I argue to the Judge that I will be representing myself because no one but me has the required underlying knowledge to do so. "The man who represents himself at trial, has a fool for a client," says the Judge. Reluctantly, the man in the black robe approves my request.

I hit the books and call as many attorneys as I know. They of course, give me free advice.

I subpoena the arresting officer, his supervisor and his field training Officer, who is most likely to be me. Then another subpoena to the regional manager. That's when the work starts.

The trial date arrives. I know that the arresting officer will tell the truth, as will his supervisor, and of course me, the field training officer. (I am both a material witness and a defendant.) I am also aware that the regional manager will not be comfortable in a courtroom setting, because he is not accustomed to telling the truth. He will not provide concise answers because his only reference material is the regulation pamphlet. He takes the stand covered with what looks like finely shredded bits of paper. He knows I will ask what documents he has been shredding. The anticipation is killing him. He knows he is beat. On the witness stand he loosens his tie and barfs.

Then my ace in the whole. I will get entered into evidence the recreational fishing regulation pamphlet itself. Defense exhibit, one and only! I will pick it apart, piece by piece, exposing everything that I have mentioned in this book. I will have leeway from the judge because he knows I'm not a real lawyer.

The prosecutor will try to object because I'm kicking his ass. "OVERULED" the Judge yells.

Then closing arguments:

"Ladies and gentlemen of the jury, I submit to you the 2022, Washington Recreational Fishing Pamphlet. Take it into deliberations with you. I ask only, that you each read it carefully and ask yourself one question and one question only. Is it ambiguous?

"If you find one ambiguous statement contained within, only one, you must hold the state accountable, DO NOT further victimize the poor fisherman! (Dramatic pause). If it doesn't fit, you must acquit!"

(Of course I made sure that there are several non-English speaking members on the jury who love to harvest sea weed, and one other outright poacher.)

Not guilty is the verdict! An acquittal is prima facie evidence of false arrest!

Then the civil litigation starts. Defamation, slander, retaliation, failure to train, pain and suffering, the list is endless. All of which require a far lesser burden of proof than at a criminal trial "preponderance of the evidence only." Of course I do not sue the officers because they had no say in making these regulations. In fact they join me, and become plaintiffs themselves.

We collect millions!

I buy a private island in Alaska, fish for Washington produced salmon till my heart's content, all the while applying the catch and release principles that I have always practiced.

But best of all, the sport fishing pamphlet in Washington State suddenly becomes a reasonable and worthwhile document. The quality of life is improved for thousands of anglers.

Alas, it is only a day dream, and the reality remains. Thank God for my private pond filled with non-native fish, bullfrogs, and trout that I planted. I am far luckier than most.

(45)

A polite letter to the WDFW commission sent upon my retirement, 2019.

From: Greg Haw (Retired Fish and Wildlife Officer)

To: WDFW Commission Chairman Larry Carpenter

Subject: Request

Dear Sir: We have met several times at commission meetings. I just retired from WDFW after 39 years. Prior to that I also held numerous temporary positions as a fisheries technician. I had a wonderful career and in fact I am a second generation F&W retiree.

I am no writer but have recently self-published a book describing 34 years as a Fish and Wildlife Officer. My duty stations included Forks, Seattle, and Olympia. I have an uncommon knowledge of enforcement work balanced equally between fisheries and game issues. I know of no one who can match my experience.

My enforcement and public service philosophies have evolved greatly over the years and they continue to do so. That said, being an advocate for the agency has become much more difficult in recent years. I have no answers regarding the hot button issues that you and yours deal with every day. But I have many suggestions regarding one issue which is "hot button" for me. I'm talking about ambiguous recreational fishing regulations, primarily those involving marine fish. Towards the end of my career I could rationalize NOT citing almost every violator due to obvious problems with published regulations. Fisheries managers refuse to seek out or even consult with officers prior to publishing rules. All of my many attempts to reach out to these folks have failed. A PDR would make this point decisively. The ONLY frustration I have had in my career is in trying to simplify regulations. West side Regional Directors were a roadblock. They simply cannot grasp the law enforcement or the recreational angling perspective. The problem is they think they do.

Numerous press releases have been distributed by WDFW over the years that acknowledge regulatory ambiguities. Any one or all could be entered into evidence as a defense exhibit in a trial. Courts are reluctant to take criminal fish and wildlife cases as a result. The RCW's and WAC's are fairly clear, it's the regulation pamphlet itself, combined with the agencies admission that they are ambiguous, that the courts object too.

WDFW is losing much needed license revenue from lost license sales as a result. The shame of it is, it all could be fixed with a stroke a pen. (Perhaps many strokes, but with a pen none the less.) No new legislation or WAC promulgation required! The many examples include regulations, the purpose for which, no longer, or perhaps never existed.

I am asking of you a favor. Could you please read my chapter "Bad Regulations?" (Enclosed) I owe you the courtesy of a preview prior to distribution. My target audience are recreational fishing / hunting groups, tackle shops, sportsman's shows...all the standard venues.

If I could help simplify recreational regulations in retirement, after failing to do so while getting paid to try, my career as a public servant would be complete.

Respectfully Greg Haw

I received a verbal response from the commission chair. He agreed with everything I wrote, but did nothing. In fact the next regulation pamphlet outlawed the possession of frozen herring in Hood Canal! (Ironically, he promoted himself to the public as a person knowledgeable about salmon fishing. Unbelievably, this man was the most knowledgeable member of the commission.)

Codicil

As mentioned prior, there are many other errors and contradictions contained within the 2022 Washington sport fishing and hunting regulation pamphlets. My attempts to point them all out ended with the realization that it would not make for interesting reading, nor would it make my points any better. Only this past week, (August 22, 2022) WDFW advertised the salmon fishing opener for the Puyallup River. On that very day, it also advertised it as closed! Realizing their mistake, and aware of the potential fallout with a powerful co manager, the Puyallup Tribe, a special detail of enforcement officers were dispatched to deal with the many anglers who were tricked into going fishing that day. Experience had taught the officers that WDFW often makes this kind of mistake, so no one was arrested to my knowledge. However many anglers, some in possession of salmon, were warned under threat of citation. I don't know about the reader, but that would ruin my entire week!

This week, WDFW errored and closed all salmon fishing in Marine Area 13. This is an area heavily advertised by WDFW as "Open year round." They did so in spite of high abundance of hatchery chinook and coho and zero wild fish interception issuers. A week later, they acknowledged their error and many folks like me had to "eat" prepaid moorage fees and hard earned vacation time. Despite the closure, the Nisqually River remained "Open" which is a main chinook producer in the area!

It is clear to me, based upon the clear ambiguity contained within the fishing and hunting regulations in Washington State, as well as the continued incompetence demonstrated in regulating our precious natural resources, that the multitude of rules on the books really don't matter. If they were important, one would think, more value would have been placed upon getting them right, and some degree of oversight would have been imposed. If these laws were thought out by real professionals, I could look back upon my thirty four year enforcement career with a much greater sense of pride.

It is my opinion that most but not all, current enforcement officers with more than about 12 years' experience, believe similarly! Almost all that don't, are upper level supervisors who do not deal directly with the public, but feel that they must maintain friendly relationships with resource managers. Therefore, officer's complaints about "Bad Regulations" are buried at the Sergeant or Captain(s) level and the folks that actually write "Bad Regulations" stay well insulated from any fallout. The Wildlife Commission simply does not care and are too busy with wolves, butterflies, and implementing Governor Inslee's anti-hunting-fishing agenda. Therein lies the problem with the working culture at the Washington Department of Fish and Wildlife.

Epilogue

Upon reading this book, the sceptic may think that the contents reflect the disjointed ramblings of a disgruntled employee. Not so. I had a wonderful career. I had priceless experiences and made many lifelong friends. I would not trade careers with any man or woman. Simply put, I did not work a day of my 39 years with WDFW. It was all play for me.

Never, even when sick, going through a divorce, or even when the Husky football team lost, did I not want to go to work. It was all a very pleasant blur.

Prospective F&W officers should not take what I write as a deterrent to a fish and wildlife enforcement career. In fact, they should think of it as job security. Never before, has the worlds need for environmental law enforcement been greater.

Each and every page on the current regulation pamphlet brings with it more and more ambiguity. Specific regulations pertaining to specific bodies of water, for the most part, have been left out of this book. Many other rules exist in the WACs (rules) that did not even make it into the regulation pamphlet. In fact there is a warning to that affect in the first paragraph of the regulation pamphlet on page one.

I have left out of this book many regulatory ambiguities and contradictions in the interest of avoiding redundancy.

When the WDFW actually gets around to fixing a regulation, it seems that the corrections made involve more confusing language rather than less. This can't continue.

Barring sweeping legislation, it is my suggestion that enforcement officers play a much larger role in the regulation process. Not just any officers, but those representing varied regions who are aware of local issues, have the proper hunting/fishing perspective, and who's true interest is with improved compliance, not with making arrests.

Nearly forty years ago, I found myself issuing a citation to a very young man near the Olympic Peninsula town of Forks Washington. It was for something minor, but I don't recall what it was for. I handed him the ticket and he said something that I will always remember, but at the time I did not recognize it for the pure truth that is was. He said, "*Thanks for the one day supply of butt wipe.*" I handed him a copy of the regulation pamphlet for future reference which was my policy at the time. He then said, "*Thanks for the three day supply of butt wipe.*"

I think about that young man often. It is my hope that he reads this. Never before have those words been more genuine or appropriate. Young folks can be remarkably wise at times.

 I dedicate this book, in part, to him.

Currently, because of policy makers, the publics respect for law enforcement in general, has never been lower. It has only one direction that it can go now. Only today did I hear that many of last year's police reform laws were rescinded by the governor. Don't forget he signed them all into law in the first place. Then today's bad news. The annual spring bear hunt was rescinded by the WDFW commissioners, appointed by the same guy. I assure you that many bear depredation permits will be granted to the timber companies as a direct result. (And they target juveniles and breeding females.)

Many of the frustrations of the outdoor enthusiasts in Washington State can be blamed on politics. Ironically, they are caused by the political side that claims to be the most environmentally conscientious.

Shame on the progressive thinking politicians who flood the world with new laws and at the same time take away our abilities to enforce them. Ignominy is due those that emphasize the "*best the available science*," then twist bad science to suit them, and use it for monetary, political or personal gain. Disgraceful are those WDFW commissioners and managers who place the outdoor enthusiast at risk of criminal or civil prosecution due to their own indifference.

Fisheries management remains a very complicated endeavor. However, there are many problems that can be easily solved with a stroke of a pen.

Let's start there!

The outdoor enthusiast in the state of Washington is clearly regulated far beyond that of his or her contemporaries in other states.

An old timer once pulled me aside and flatly stated: *"We have by far the most complicated regulation pamphlet in the United States of America. You have got to be a lawyer to figure it out, and even then it's difficult."*

I said to the old timer that he couldn't be more wrong! A scowl crossed his face in pure disbelief. I said: *"We have the six most complicated regulation pamphlets in America, and what's more, there is not a lawyer on earth that can make any sense out of any of them!"* (The gentleman had forgotten about small game, turkey regulations, waterfowl, big game, and yes, the gold panning regulation pamphlet! Yes, WDFW regulates gold panning too!)

It is very difficult for the outdoor enthusiast in Washington State to not be depressed at times. However, this depression is occasionally lifted by biological accidents and even escaped Atlantic salmon! The fact is, that if we didn't have salmon and trout hatcheries, we would have almost nothing but non-native fish species to lawfully fish. WDFW has managed more species to the brink of extinction than any conservation agency on earth!

Waiting around for wild salmon stocks to naturally recover is the dream of idealists, not realists.

Wild salmon populations have taken a nose dive despite decades of habitat improvement projects and millions of wasted dollars. Removing dams does not spontaneously produce wild stocks of salmon although WDFW managers apparently believe in the ancient scientific myth of *spontaneous generation*. Even endangered species like the beloved orca, are crying out for more hatchery chinook production, while the anti-hatchery proponents are ironically, successful in their efforts to starve them out!

An old family friend, and true salmon advocate once told me: *"It cost 400 million dollars to remove the Elwha dams, and we still need a hatchery there. Cutting the commercial troll fishery for a week would have saved far more wild fish, and it would have been free."*

Occasional biological accidents make a bad thing slightly better, but it seems that every intended improvement fails.

The outdoor enthusiasts in the great state of Washington need to ask themselves, *"How did things get so screwed up?"* All of the issues detailed within this book represent only a small fraction of what is wrong with the WDFW. What I truly do not understand is why others within the agency are not making similar points as me. Do they think that all is well?

In recent years there have been many well-known allegations of sexual harassment and workplace bullying at WDFW. There have been well-documented wrongful terminations and quite a few cases where public disclosure requests were fouled up, resulting in thousands of dollars in fines, paid for by the tax payer with no repercussions placed on those responsible. There have been cases where employees have tried to speak out about wrongdoing, only to be *"forced out"* for speaking out. I must admit, that while an employee of the WDFW, I would not have dreamed of speaking out in this manner. Yes, I believe that I too, would have been *"forced out,"* had I done so. This should not be the case.

Even I felt compelled to wait three years after retirement to write down many of these thoughts, such was my conditioning after 39 years with WDFW.

Yes, I believe that the workplace culture within this agency is a large part of the problem. Failures are rewarded, and no one in the agency, it seems, is aware of how success should be measured.

One would think, by looking at the recent record, that success is measured by how many recreational fishing and hunting opportunities can be taken away, or by how many species can be listed under ESA. I see their results as total failures.

Enforcement officers are doing their best, but due to the current state of affairs with **WDFW**, success is illusive.

If what I have written here seems personal, if not a little hostile, well... it is! My entire working life was motivated by the vision of a long and happy retirement focusing upon things that I love to do with the people that love to do them with me. This sentiment is shared by many. The truly sad part is that young folks, never exposed to what once was, will never know what could be. I believe that if things don't drastically change, and quickly, an entire way of life for the outdoor enthusiast will be gone forever.

The buck stops with the current Governor, his wildlife commission and their puppet director.

Enough said.

The End

Glossary of terms used (Authors intent)

Ambiguity: When a single word or phrase may be interpreted in two or more ways.

Adam Henry, A-Hole, Anti-hatchery advocates: Unrealistic folks that believe that all dams should be removed and rivers will be someday rerouted. Spawning gravel will replace itself, culverts will restore wild stocks, and that wild fish currently exist in numbers that will repopulate themselves. They believe that an additional gas tax in Washington will solve global climate change and that commercial fisheries impacting wild fish make sense. They believe that throwing money at environmental issues, with no oversight will change their world, and crimes should go unpunished even the ones they invent. (And that all drugs should be legal. Convenient perhaps?)

Bad Regulations: A very high percentage of regulatory demands placed upon outdoor enthusiasts by WDFW. Often discriminatory to race, or to those with lower economic status.

Bad Regulation Deniers: Typically, only those that write them, or those that are in a position that they must defend them because their subordinates wrote them. (Less than .0000000842 percent of the population.)

Bandit: A fisher or hunter who does so with an intent to violate the regulations.

Bird cage liner: Pages of the Washington fishing regulation pamphlet. AKA butt wipe.

Bio...Biologist: Those holding that title that work for the Washington State Department of Fish and Wildlife.

BPA: Bonneville Power Administration.

Bug: Once an affectionate term for a professional fisheries or game biologist. Now a derogatory term. (Rarely used anymore.)

Bucket Biologist: Motivated by poor state fish management, a person who takes it upon himself to improve fishing opportunity in Washington State, and often succeeds. He or she, transports self-caught fish and introduces them to other bodies of water where they do not naturally belong. A crime, with often wonderful results.

Butt Wipe: Any of the 150 pages of the current recreational fishing regulation pamphlet.

Cheat / Cheater: Anglers with lawful intent, who are often confused enough by the law to find themselves in violation of some hidden technicality. (Just about all of us.)

Commissioner: One of nine members of the Washington State Wildlife Commission. Appointed by the Governor and approved by the legislature. (Well, that is the law, but it is often ignored.)

Director: Appointed by the commission. By law, responsible for conservation, wise use, protection of and enhancement of recreational and commercial fishing opportunities.

Double blind index: An experimental control mechanism where participants in an experimental study are allocated to groups according to a random algorithm.

Emergency WAC: A sudden knee jerk reaction, (rule change) caused by both anticipated and unanticipated events. Often given by very short notice or none at all, and with often dubious justification.

Equitable Estoppel: A judicial doctrine, a legal concept supported by case law. As used in this document it means, simply, any ambiguity in written form, must be applied in favor of the party that did not create the ambiguity. (See disclaimer)

ESA: Endangered Species Act. (Ironically, wild salmon stocks have taken a nose dive since this was enacted.)

Fish Cop: Current Fish and Wildlife Officer, but more accurately refers to a fisheries officer prior to merger of fish and game. (Before 1994)

Fish Hog: An angler obsessed with take. Motivated by greed. Does not practice catch and release unless forced to do so by law, and even then, only when someone is looking.

Fishing license / permit: A document issued (sold) by WDFW to allow for take, access, or opportunity, whether real or imagined.

Fish Cop / Game Warden: aka fish and wildlife police officer, Greene Meany, mallard marshal, creek dick, water Nazi: Authorized state peace officer assigned to enforce all criminal laws of the State of Washington. Also federally commissioned.

Flosser: An angler that has discovered a way to beat the anti-snagging rules.

Food fish: Fish or shellfish species that may be commercially harvested. However treaty Indian fishing allows for the take of game fish for commercial purposes. (This concept makes no sense and serves no purpose.)

FTO: Field training officer.

Food Fish: Fish and shellfish that are commercially and recreationally regulated. (Including many that are not.) The term, although defined by law, serves no purpose.

Game Fish: May only be harvested for recreational fishing. (This concept is ignored by WDFW when it involves treaty tribal fishing or cultured game fish species. It makes no sense nor serves any purpose.)

Indian basher: Those that wrongly blame treaty Indian fishing rights as the cause of the current state of affairs with fish and wildlife management. (Often times they don't understand that treaty Indian fishing laws are our only possible salvation.)

Line pusher: An angler that pushes fishing boundary lines to the point that it draws the attention of the fish cop.

Marine Area: Specific marine areas as defined by law, each with different fishing regulations. (Numbered 1 through 13 with many sub groups. Too many to number here.)

Meat liner: An unlawful fishing tactic where an angler surreptitiously attaches extra, unlawful sets of terminal tackle to the mainline of his seemingly lawful gear.

Non-native species: Fish and wildlife living in a wild state that were introduced by artificial means and directly compete with native species. All have a negative effect, yet many provide recreation and other benefits. They include, but are not limited to almost all freshwater game fish, many species of game birds, and some big game species.

Poacher: A wildlife thief.

Regional Director: Acts on the directors behalf on a regional level. There are six total, one per region. Although in the author's experience, their true role is unknown.

RCW: State Law (Revised Code of Washington.)

Recreational fishing regulation pamphlet: A publication distributed by the WDFW in an attempt to gain compliance with hunting and fishing regulations. It very often times has the opposite effect.

Tree hugger, anti-hunter, anti-fisher, anti-trapper, anti-bait, unclassified marine invertebrate enthusiast, wolf lover, anti-second amendment, bird watcher etc. etc.: Those opposed to hunting and fishing in general, but they believe that they are not. Unrealistic in their beliefs, and woefully ignorant of real biological issues, despite their education. The contents of this book is a complete shock to them! An apparent requirement for appointment to the WDFW Commission.

Snagger: An angler attempting to impale a fish on a hook without the fish biting a bait or lure. Not necessarily a violation of law.

Strict liability: A legal concept applied in both criminal and civil law that holds a defendant responsible for their actions regardless of their intent at the time of the action. (Fish and wildlife violations fall into this category.)

Turd Burglar: A WDFW marine mammal expert who collects fecal samples from orca, in an attempt to prove that Orca eat only chinook salmon. **AKA Federal Grant Seeker.**

Unclassified marine invertebrate: Just about everything that does not live on land, and a few that do. Includes microbes, and single celled organisms. (Unlawful to possess)

WAC: Washington Administrative Code. State rules, supported by RCW.

WDFW: Washington Department of Fish and Wildlife. AKA Washington Department of Failed Wildlife, Wash Dept. of %$&*@# -UP Wildlife.

Wildlife: Any animal that lives in a wild state. (Includes non-native species)

Acknowledgements

Once again much thanks is due my daughter Melissa Morrison who patiently assisted me with many technical issues.

Thanks are due to my wife of 15 years Crissy, who tolerated me while I was cursing at the computer screen.

To Dave Young, Mark Johnson and Danny Boldt. Old friends, fishing buddies and many shared memories.

My brother Mike, although infinitely annoying regarding editing issues, he was usually right. Mom and Dad were a great help too. (Although neither agreed with all I had to say, or how I said it.)

My thanks to numerous, current Fish and Wildlife Officers, who tolerated me as a trainer, even if they, at times, did not agree with me. Game Warden Hall of Fame member Calvin Tresser, encouraged me to keep writing at a point where I wanted to quit. Sergeant Brian Fairbanks (retired) provided valuable insights and welcome feedback, both good and bad.

This author was honored to have the Honorable Gary W. Velie write a forward for this book. Clallam County Superior Court Judge (Retired), and a former Fish and Wildlife Officer himself. He did so without hesitation. He is a true champion of law and order, but most of all, an angler.

Bobbi Monk, who to me and many others, was a consistent and very positive presence in Fish and Wildlife Enforcement Office for many years. She assisted me in more ways than she knows.

Last but not least, I wish to acknowledge all of my small boat fishing friends that I recognize only by the shape of their boats. (Pisser, Leaky Lemon, Stretch, Kelly C., Pirate Bob, Long Rod Larry, Stinky Jim, the Jerk, Wrong Way, Big Tom and his disciples, and many others.)

To All, Thank You!

Greg Haw Signing Out

A proud group, rich in history, highly trained and well vetted, whose skills are wasted by those who write the laws.

About the author

Greg Haw started his career with the Washington Department of Fisheries as a fisheries technician and fish culturist at several salmon hatcheries. He began his law enforcement career in 1985 and was assigned to the Forks, Washington duty station. Later, he did a short stint in Seattle, and then spent 30 plus years stationed in Olympia patrolling primarily the Olympic Peninsula and the Puget Sound area. With the merger of the Department of Game with the Department of Fisheries, he became a Fish and Wildlife Officer and continued his patrol work until 2019 when he retired.

He received many awards for his patrol work, and was heavily involved with training new officers the last twenty years or so of his career. Until the very end, he tried very hard to advocate for recreational anglers and especially to simplify fishing and hunting regulations. He failed.

Since his retirement Greg has written three books reminiscing upon his career as a Fish and Wildlife Enforcement Officer and on the absurdity of the current fishing regulations. He remains hopeful that he can accomplish in retirement, that which he couldn't accomplish when getting paid to try.

Dedication

This publication is dedicated to all outdoor enthusiasts that have been cited, pinched, inconvenienced or busted, for overly complex fishing regulations that were poorly worded, didn't make sense or were suddenly imposed without good reason: and especially for those so treated, while making a conscientious attempt to follow the rules.

 I especially wish to thank that young man out in Forks that I cited those many years ago, the one who said, "Thanks for the three day supply of butt wipe."

This dedication specifically excludes intentional violators, poachers, jack lighters, party hunters, fish hogs, sign shooters, litter bugs, bandits, line pushers, flossers, bandits, tribal fishing bashers, meat liners, two trippers, Fish and Wildlife Commissioners and autocrats, "bad regulation" deniers, or folks that hide clams in hip boots.

Or those who blame the fish cop for this mess.

Other titles by Haw, available on Amazon
Books

Confessions of an Urban Fish and Wildlife
Officer in Washington State

Confessions of a Washington Game Warden

Book II